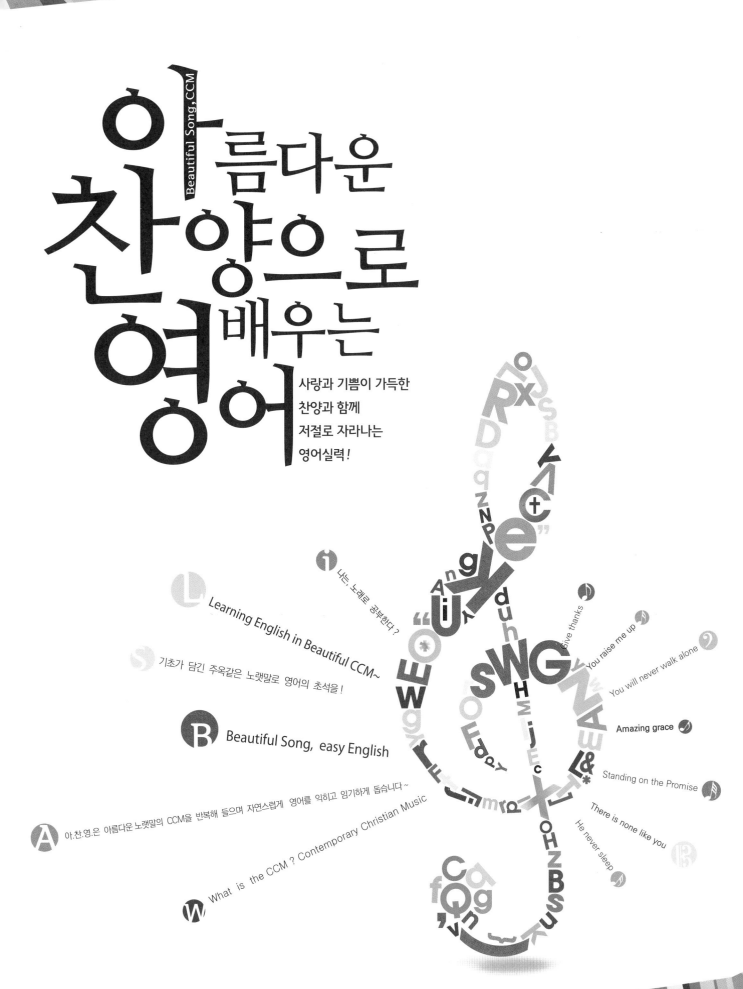

Prologue

초 등학생 딸과 아들이 기쁘게 영어공부를 할 수 있으면 해서 이 책을 쓰기 시작하였고 그 과정에서 딸과 아들이 많은 내용을 아이들의 눈높이에서 지적해주어 이를 반영하여 이 책을 집필하였습니다. 그리고 감리교신학대학교 박은영 영어담당 교수님이 이 책의 많은 부분을 수정해주시고 지도해 주셨으며 끊임없이 격려해주셔서 이 책을 완성하였습니다.

아 이들의 눈높이로 노래를 선곡하여 너무 슬프거나 영어 가사가 어려운 노래는 제외하고 밝고 아름다운 노래 위주로 그리고 초등학교 고학년에서 중학교 학생 수준에 맞추어 영어 찬양을 선곡하였습니다. 그리고 가능하면 난이도가 쉬운 노래부터 어려운 노래 순으로 배울 수 있도록 하였습니다.

무 엇보다도 기존의 영어 교육 교재들이 많은 내용과 연습문제 등으로 공부하는 학생들을 힘들게 만드는 면이 있으나 이 책에서는 가능한 편안하고 기쁘게 영어를 배울 수 있도록 하였습니다.

우 리나라 사람들이 영어에 투입하는 시간이 많으나 효과가 높지 않은 이유 중 하나가 계속해서 다른 것을 공부한다는데 있습니다. 영어는 지속적인 반복을 통하여 기본적인 틀을 암기하고 그 암기했던 것을 바탕으로 점점 영역을 넓혀 가는 것이 중요합니다. 그래서 많은 전문가들이 권하는 것은 영어의 기본이 되는 영어 속담, 또는 잘 알려진 영어 노래를 외우는 것입니다. 이를 통하여 기본적인 단어와 문장을 모두 알 수 있고 영미권 사람들의 기본적인 사고방식 또한 알 수 있게 되어 영어 독해가 쉬워집니다. 그래서 예문으로 가능하면 많은 서양 명언과 속담을 포함하였습니다.

이 책에서는 영어가사를 가능하면 직역을 하여 정확한 뜻의 전달과 영어 공부를 할 수 있도록 하였습니다. 영어가사를 한글로 의역하면 더 아름답게 의미가 전달될 수 있지만, 한글 의역을 통한 노래의 의미 파악보다는 영어 그대로의 느낌을 살리면서 노래를 들어보고 해석해 보는 것이 영어를 공부한다는 차원에서 바람직하기 때문입니다.

주 일학교에서 이 책을 교재로 사용한다면 노래 듣기와 해석을 통한 공부에 1~2주, 목사님이나 전도사님이 관련 성경말씀을 강의해 주시고 노래와 친해지는데 1주일, 그리고 아이들이 파트를 나누어서 직접 노래 해보고 노래와 관련된 성경말씀에 대해 서로의 체험(간증) 나누기를 1주일 정도 한다면 한 달에 CCM(Contemporary Christian Music) 1개를 배울 수 있어 1년 동안 12개 정도의 CCM을 배울 수 있을 것입니다.

물 론 교회나 성당을 다니지 않는다 하더라도 아름다운 영어가사와 선율로 이루어진 하나님을 향한 사랑의 노래인 CCM을 반복해서 듣고 저절로 외우면서 편안하고 행복하게 영어를 배울 수 있을 것입니다.

대 부분 아이들이 초등학생 시절이 지나면 질풍노도의 시기를 겪게 됩니다. 북한이 우리나라를 쳐들어오지 못하는 것은 4차원의 중학생들이 있기 때문이라는 말이 있을 정도입니다. 그러나 초등학생 시절부터 지극한 선이신 주님의 영향력 안에서 하나님이 주신 달란트를 갈고 닦으며 청소년기를 보낸다면 이 땅의 청소년들 각자가 행복하고 즐거운 삶을 살 수 있을 것이며 우리나라도 정말 더욱 아름답고 훌륭한 나라가 될 수 있다고 생각됩니다.

마 지막으로 성령의 영감으로 이렇게 아름다운 곡들을 세상에 나오게 해주신 이 곡들의 작사가, 작곡가와 찬양사역자분들께 감사드리며 영원토록 찬양받으실 하나님께 모든 영광을 돌립니다.

이철주 올림

About this book

~~이 책의 구성은...~~

아래와 같이 노래를 알아보고, 노래를 배워보고,
번역해본 후 관련된 성경 말씀을 알아보도록
구성되어 있습니다.

Draw me close to you

Draw me close to You
Never let me go
I lay it all down again
To hear You say that I'm Your friend

⋮

> ◇ QR코드를 스캔하여 유튜브로 들어보세요!!
> ◇ 유튜브(www.youtube.com) 검색창에 아래와 같이 입력하고 돋보기를
>   클릭해도 됩니다.
>
> | draw me close michael w smith | 🔍 |

⋮

 ## 노래 알아보기

이곡은 작곡가이고, 키보드 연주자이며, 예배 인도 사역자인 켈리 카펜터(Kelly carpenter)가 1994년에 작곡 하였습니다. 켈리
카펜터는 어느 날 모든 것을 내려놓고 주님과 가까워지고자 하는 기도 후에 20분 정도의 짧은 ...

⋮

 ## 노래 배우기

Draw me close to You

draw (~을) 끌다, 잡아당기다, 뽑아내다	▶**drawer** 서랍
close (시간이나 거리가) 가까운, 이웃한, 친밀한	▶**close to** ~~로 가까이

▶near도 가까운 이란 뜻인데 close는 near보다 더 가까울 때 사용됩니다

⋮

🎵 노래 배우기(REmind)

Draw me close to You

draw _____끌다_____ ▶ **drawer**_____서랍_____
close _____가까이_____ ▶ **close to**_____~로 가까이_____ ▶ **near** _____가까운_____

⋮

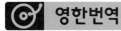

영한번역

Draw me close to You
Never let me go
I lay it all down again
To hear You say that I'm Your friend

> 나를 이끌어 주세요 당신(하나님)께로
> 나를 가도록 하지 말아 주세요
> 나는 다시 그 모든 것을 내려놓습니다
> 당신이 '내가 당신의 친구'라고 말씀하시는 것을 듣기 위하여
> ⋮

번역해보기

Draw me close to You   _나를 이끌어 주세요 당신(하나님)께로_
Never let me go   _____
I lay it all down again   _____
To hear You say that I'm Your friend   _____
⋮

노래와 관련된 성경 말씀   앞서 배운 영어찬양과 관련된 성경말씀을 알아봅시다!!

"No one can come to me unless the Father who sent me draws him, and I will raise him up at the last day.
(John 6:44)

나를 보내신 아버지께서 이끌지 아니하시면 아무도 내게 올 수 없으니 오는 그를 내가 마지막 날에 다시 살리리라. (요한복음 6:44)
⋮

영어성경 말씀을 한글로 해석해 보기

"No one can come to me unless the Father who sent me draws him, and I will raise him up at the last day.
(John 6:44)

_____

이 책에서는 기호를 사용하여...

관련 영어 단어를 암기하기 쉽도록 하였고 듣기에 도움을 주고자 발음에 관한 기호를 표시였습니다.
이 책에 나오는 기호들은 아래와 같습니다.

기 호	예 문
↔ 반의어(반대말)	near 가까운, 가까이 ↔ far 먼, 멀리
= 동의어(또는 유의어)	grateful 감사하는 (=thankful)
< 부등호는 더 강한 의미임을 나타낼 때	desire 열망, 간절히 원하다 > want 바라는 것, 원하다
[ ] 발음	I'll [아이월]이 아닌 [아일]이라고 발음됩니다
▶ 관련 단어, 숙어 또는 예문	with ~을 가지고, 와 함께 ▶ with water 물을 가지고 ▶ with me 나와 함께
속담 관련된 속담(proverb)	속담 A friend in need is a friend indeed 필요할 때 친구가 진정한 친구

이 책에 수록된 곡들은...

QR코드를 스캔하여 유튜브(www.youtube.com)에서 들어볼 수 있습니다. 물론 직접 유튜브(www.youtube.com)에 접속하여 CCM을 찾아 들어보면 여러 찬양사역자들이 부른 다양한 버전을 들어볼 수 있어 좋습니다.

이 책에 수록된 성경은...

한글은 개역개정, 영문은 NIV(new international version)를 사용하였습니다.

C·O·N·T·E·N·T·S

Draw me close to you*

Draw me close to You
Never let me go
I lay it all down again
To hear You say that I'm Your friend

You are my desire
No one else will do
Cause nothing else could take Your place

To feel the warmth of Your embrace
Help me find the way
Bring me back to You

You're all I want
You're all I've ever needed
You're all I want
Help me know You are near

◇ QR코드를 스캔하여 유튜브로 들어보세요!!

◇ 유튜브(www.youtube.com) 검색창에 아래와 같이 입력하고 돋보기를 클릭해도 됩니다.

| draw me close michael w smith | 🔍 |

노래 알아보기

이곡은 작곡가이고, 피아니스트이며, 예배 인도 사역자인 켈리 카펜터(Kelly Carpenter)가 1994년에 작곡하였습니다. 켈리 카펜터는 어느 날 모든 것을 내려놓고 주님과 가까워지고자 하는 기도후에 20분 정도의 짧은 시간동안 이 노래를 작곡했다고 합니다. 이곡은 세상에 나온 후 한동안은 많이 알려지지 않았지만 목사이자 찬양사역자인 앤디 팍(Andy Park)과 5인의 형제로 이루어진 그룹인 더 카티나스(The Katinas)가 부르면서 알려지기 시작했고, 특히 마이클 더블유 스미스(Michael W. Smith)가 2001년 발표한 앨범인 워쉽(Worship)에 이 곡이 수록되면서 많이 알려지게 되었습니다. 피아노 반주와 잘 어울리고 노래가 어렵지 않으며 감미롭고 포근한 느낌의 노래입니다.

♪ 노래 배우기

Draw me close to You

draw (~을) 끌다, 잡아당기다, 뽑아내다, (그림을) 그리다 ▶ **drawer** 서랍
close (시간이나 거리가) 가까운, 이웃한, 친밀한
  ▶ **close to** ~ ~로 가까이
  ▶ near도 가까운 이란 뜻인데 close는 near보다 더 가까울 때 사용됩니다

Never let me go

never 절대(결코, 한 번도) ~ 않다
let me ~ 내가 ~ 하도록 해주세요(하소서)
  ▶ let me introduce myself 제 소개를 하게 해주세요
go 가다 (go-went-went)

I lay it all down again

lay ~ down ~을 내려놓다 (lay-layed-lain)
again 다시, 한번 더

To hear You say that I'm Your friend

hear (소리를)듣다, (소리가)들리다
  ▶ I stopped singing to hear the sound 나는 그 소리를 듣기 위해 노래하기를 멈추었다
  ▶ Can you hear? 들리니?
say 말하다 (say-said-said)
friend 친구 ▶ 속담 A friend in need is a friend indeed 필요할 때 친구가 진정한 친구

You are my desire

desire 열망, 동경, (정말로 간절히) 원하다 > want 바라는 것, 바라다, 원하다

No one else will do

else 또 다른
▶ anything else 그밖에 무언가 ▶ something else 무언가 다른 중요한 것
do 하다 (do-did-done)

Cause nothing else could take Your place

cause 왜냐하면(=because)
nothing else 다른 아무것도
take 가져가다, 데리고 가다, 가지다, 필요로 하다 (take-took-taken)
take your 두 단어를 붙여서 [테이켤]이라고 발음합니다
place 장소, 자리, 지위, 위치
take one's place 누구를 대신하다

To feel the warmth of Your embrace

feel 느끼다 ▶ to feel 느끼기 위해서 ▶ feeling 느낌
warmth 온기, 체온 ▶ warm 따뜻한
embrace 포옹(= hug)

Help me find the way

help 도와주다, 도움 ▶ pray to God for help 하나님께 도움을 구하다
find (우연히) 찾다 ▶ find out 발견하다, 알아내다, 간파하다
way 길, 방법
▶ 속담 Where there is a will, there is a way 뜻이 있는 곳에 길이 있다

Bring me back to You

bring 가져오다 ▶ bring me my bag 나에게 내 가방을 가져다줘
back 뒤로, 등, 척추, 다시 ▶ back to back 등을 마주하고
▶ get something back (잃었던 것을) 되찾다

You're all I want

you're(=you are) [유얼]에서 유가 거의 들리지 않아 [열]이라고 발음됩니다
all 모든, 모든 것, [올]보다는 [얼]에 가깝게 발음됩니다
want 바라는 것, 바라다, 원하다
all (that) I want 이 문장에서는 'that' 이 생략되어 있고 'I want'가 'all'을 꾸며주고 있습니다

You're all I've ever needed

ever 언제나, 항상, 정말로, 매우
I've(=I have) 've' 가 작게 발음되어 [아입]이라 발음됩니다
need 필요, 필요로 하다
▶ (PV) A friend in need is a friend indeed 필요할 때 친구가 진정한 친구

You're all I want
Help me know You are near
know 알다(know-knew-known) ▶ knowledge 지식
near 가까운, 가까이 ↔ far 멀리

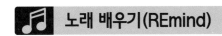 **노래 배우기(REmind)**

아래와 같이 앞서 배웠던 단어나 문구의 뜻을 말해보고 각자 문장을 만들어 보세요!!

Draw me close to You
draw _끌다_ ▶ **drawer** _서랍_
close _가까이_
　▶ **close to ~** _~로 가까이_
　▶ **near** _가까운_

Never let me go
never
let me ~
　▶ let me introduce myself
go

I lay it all down again
lay ~ down
again

To hear You say that I'm Your friend
hear
　▶ I stopped singing to hear the sound .
　▶ can you hear?
say
friend ▶ 속담 A friend in _____ is a friend indeed

You are my desire
desire _____ > want

No one else will do

else _____ ▶ anything else _____ ▶ something else _____ do _____

Cause nothing else could take Your place

cause(=because) _____
nothing else _____
take _____
take one's place _____

To feel the warmth of Your embrace

feel _____ ▶ to feel _____ ▶ feeling _____
warmth _____ ▶ warm _____
embrace(= _____)

Help me find the way

help _____ ▶ pray to God for help _____
find _____ ▶ find out _____
way _____

Bring me back to You

bring _____ ▶ bring me my bag _____
back _____ ▶ back to back _____
▶ get something back _____

You're all I want

all _____
want _____

You're all I've ever needed

ever _____
need _____ ▶ A friend in _____ is a friend _____

You're all I want
Help me know You are near

know _____ ▶ knowledge _____
near _____ ↔ far _____

영한번역

Draw me close to You	나를 이끌어 주세요 당신(하나님)께로
Never let me go	나를 가도록 하지 말아 주세요
I lay it all down again	나는 다시 그 모든 것을 내려놓습니다
To hear You say that I'm Your friend	당신이 '내가 당신의 친구'라고 말씀하시는 것을 듣기 위하여

You are my desire	당신(하나님)은 나의 소망
No one else will do	아무도 그렇게 할 수 없습니다
Cause nothing else could take Your place	왜냐하면 아무것도 당신의 자리를 차지(대신)할 수 없기 때문입니다
To feel the warmth of Your embrace	당신의 안아주심의 따뜻함을 느끼기 위하여
Help me find the way	내가 그 길을 찾도록 도와주세요
Bring me back to You	나를 당신께로 되돌려 주세요

You're all I want	당신(하나님)은 내가 원하는 모든 것
You're all I've ever needed	당신은 내가 정말로(언제나) 필요로 하는 모든 것
You're all I want	당신은 내가 원하는 모든 것
Help me know You are near	당신이 곁에 계시다는 것을 내가 알도록 도와주세요

* 상기 번역은 영어공부를 위한 해석(직역)이며 공인된 한글 번역곡(가사)은 아님을 알려드립니다

번역해보기

Draw me close to You　　　　　　　나를 이끌어 주세요 당신(하나님)께로

Never let me go

I lay it all down again

To hear You say that I'm Your friend

You are my desire　　　　　　　　당신은 나의 소망(열망)

No one else will do

Cause nothing else could take Your place

To feel the warmth of Your embrace

Help me find the way

Bring me back to You

You're all I want　　　　　　　　당신은 내가 원하는 모든 것

You're all I've ever needed

You're all I want

Help me know You are near

✝ 노래와 관련된 성경 말씀

앞서 배운 영어찬양과 관련된 성경말씀을 알아봅시다!!

Submit yourselves, then, to God. Resist the devil, and he will flee from you.
Come near to God and he will come near to you. Wash your hands, you sinners, and purify your hearts, you double-minded. (James 4:7-8)

그런즉 너희는 하나님께 복종할지어다 마귀를 대적하라 그리하면 너희를 피하리라. 하나님을 가까이하라 그리하면 너희를 가까이하시리라 죄인들아 손을 깨끗이 하라 두 마음을 품은 자들아 마음을 성결하게 하라.

(야고보서 4:7-8)

"Come to me, all you who are weary and burdened, and I will give you rest. (Matthew 11:28)

"수고하고 무거운 짐 진 모든 자들아, 너희는 내게로 오라. 내가 너희에게 안식을 주리라."(마태복음 11:28)

"No one can come to me unless the Father who sent me draws him, and I will raise him up at the last day. (John 6:44)

나를 보내신 아버지께서 이끌지 아니하시면 아무도 내게 올 수 없으니 오는 그를 내가 마지막 날에 다시 살리리라. (요한복음 6:44)

The reason my Father loves me is that I lay down my life-only to take it up again. (John 10:17)

내가 내 목숨을 버리는 것은 그것을 내가 다시 얻기 위함이니 이로 말미암아 아버지께서 나를 사랑하시느니라.
(요한복음 10:17)

Let us then approach God's throne of grace with confidence, so that we may receive mercy and find grace to help us in our time of need. (Hebrews 4:16)

그러므로 우리가 긍휼을 얻고 필요한 때에 도우시는 은혜를 얻기 위해 은혜의 왕좌로 담대히 갈 것이니라.
(히브리서 4:16)

But as for me, it is good to be near God. I have made the Sovereign LORD my refuge;　I will tell of all your deeds. (Psalm 73:28)

하나님께 가까이 함이 내게 복이라 내가 주 여호와를 나의 피난처로 삼아 주의 모든 행적을 전파하리이다. (시편 73:28)

Let us come before him with thanksgiving and extol him with music and song. (Psalm 95:2)

"우리가 감사하며 그분 앞에 나아가고 시를 지어 그분을 향해 즐거이 소리치자. (시편 95:2)

Worship the LORD with gladness; come before him with joyful songs. (Psalm 100:2)

"즐거움으로 주를 섬기고 노래하면서 그분 앞으로 갈지어다."(시편 100:2)

The LORD is near to all who call on him, to all who call on him in truth. (Psalms 145:18)

"여호와께서는 자기에게 간구하는 모든 자 곧 진실하게 간구하는 모든 자에게 가까이 하시는도다" (시편 145:18)

(James 4:7-8) **flee from** ~로 부터 도망가다
(John 6:44) **unless** ~ 하지 않으면
(John 10:17) **reason** 이유, 까닭 / **reasonable** 이치에 맞는, 합리적인
(Hebrews 4:16) **with confidence** 자신(확신)을 가지고
(Psalms 145:18) **in truth** 진실로, 참으로

앞서 배운 성경말씀을 소리 내어 읽어보고 해석해 보세요!!

Submit yourselves, then, to God. Resist the devil, and he will flee from you.
Come near to God and he will come near to you. Wash your hands, you sinners, and purify your hearts, you double-minded. (James 4:7-8)

"Come to me, all you who are weary and burdened, and I will give you rest. (Matthew 11:28)

"No one can come to me unless the Father who sent me draws him, and I will raise him up at the last day. (John 6:44)

The reason my Father loves me is that I lay down my life--only to take it up again. (John 10:17)

Let us then approach God's throne of grace with confidence, so that we may receive mercy and find grace to help us in our time of need. (Hebrews 4:16)

But as for me, it is good to be near God. I have made the Sovereign LORD my refuge; I will tell of all your deeds. (Psalm 73:28)

Let us come before him with thanksgiving and extol him with music and song. (Psalm 95:2)

Worship the LORD with gladness; come before him with joyful songs. (Psalm 100:2)

The LORD is near to all who call on him, to all who call on him in truth. (Psalms 145:18)

Puzzle 1

'DRAM ME CLOSE TO YOU' 에서 배웠던 단어들로 퍼즐을 완성해 봅시다!

Across_가로

1. 장소, 자리, 지위, 위치
5. 서랍
6. 지식
   ▶ A little _____ is dangerous
   얕은 지식은 위험하다, 선무당이 사람 잡는다
7. 말하다 (= talk)
8. 느끼다
9. 가까운, 가까이 (↔ far 멀리)
10. 시간이나 거리가) 가까운, 이웃한, 친밀한
12. 듣다, 들리다

Down_세로

2. 포옹(= hug)
3. 도와주다
4. 진정한
   A friend in need is a friend _____
5. 열망, 동경, (정말로 간절히) 원하다 > want
8. 친구
9. 절대(결코, 한번도)
   ▶ _____ let me go
11. (조심스럽게, 바닥에) 내려놓다
   ▶ I _____ it all down again

정답은 책의 뒤편에서 확인하세요

MEMO

Give Thanks*

Give thanks with a grateful heart
Give thanks to the Holy One
Give thanks because He's given Jesus Christ, His Son ×2

And now let the weak say, "I am strong"
Let the poor say, "I am rich"
Because of what the Lord has done for us ×2

Give thanks with a grateful heart
Give thanks to the Holy One
Give thanks because He's given Jesus Christ, His Son ×2

And now let the weak say, "I am strong"
Let the poor say, "I am rich"
Because of what the Lord has done for us ×2

Give thanks
We Give thanks ×2

◇ QR코드를 스캔하여 유튜브로 들어보세요!!
◇ 유튜브(www.youtube.com) 검색창에 아래와 같이 입력하고 돋보기를 클릭해도 됩니다.

| give thanks don moen | 🔍 |

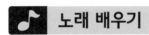 **노래 알아보기**

이곡은 작곡가 헨리 스미스(Henry Smith)가 1978년에 작곡하였습니다. 헨리 스미스는 이 곡을 작곡할 당시부터 시력을 잃어가는 병으로 눈이 점점 안 보이게 되었지만 언젠가 목사님의 설교 말씀 중 들었던 고린도 후서 8장 9절의 말씀이 계속 마음속에 떠올라 주님에 대한 변함없는 감사와 사랑의 고백으로 이 곡을 작곡하게 되었다 합니다. 우리나라에서는 돈 모엔(Don Moen) 목사님이 부르신 노래로 널리 알려져 있는데, 이곡은 돈 모엔(Don Moen) 목사님이 최초로 녹음한 라이브 찬양앨범이며 1986년에 발표된 같은 이름의 앨범(Give Thanks)에 타이틀곡으로 수록되어 있습니다. 또한 여러 국가의 언어로 번역되어 전 세계적으로 널리 알려진 찬양입니다. 우리나라에서는 '거룩하신 하나님'이라는 곡으로 많이 불리고 있습니다.

노래 배우기

Give thanks with a grateful heart

Give thanks 감사를 주어라(=감사드리자)
with ~을 가지고, 와 함께 ▶ with water 물을 가지고 ▶ with me 나와 함께
grateful(=thankful, glad) 감사하는, 고마워하는, 기쁜
heart 마음, 심장

Give thanks to the Holy One

thanks to ~ ~에게 감사하다
holy 거룩한 ▶ silent night holy night 고요한 밤 거룩한 밤 ▶ holiness 거룩함
one 존재, 하나, 한 개

Give thanks because He's given Jesus Christ, His Son

because 때문에
He 그, 여기서는 대문자로 하나님을 뜻함
He's given(= He has given) [히스기븐]이라 들립니다
give 주다(give-gave-given)
Jesus Christ 예수님
His 하나님의 ▶ His Son(=Jesus Christ) 하나님의 아들
Jesus Christ와 His Son 사이의 컴마(,)는 동등한 것을 연결할 때 사용됩니다

And now let the weak say, "I am strong"

and 그리고 ↔ but 그러나
now 지금 ▶ past 과거 ▶ future 미래
let 허락하다, 시키다
▶ let me drink water 내가 물을 먹도록 허락해 주세요
weak 약한
▶ the weak 약한 사람들
say 말하다(say-said-said)
strong 강한, 힘쎈 ▶ strength 힘
▶ 속담 In unity, there is strength 뭉치는 곳에 힘이 있다

Let the poor say, "I am rich"

poor 가난한 ▶ the poor 가난한 사람들
rich 부유한 ▶ the rich 부유한 사람들
'the + 형용사'는 '형용사 성질을 가진 사람들'로 해석합니다

Because of what the Lord has done for us

because (of) 때문에 ▶ because 뒤에는 문장이 because of 뒤에는 명사 또는 명사절이 옵니다
what ~한 것, ~한 일, 무엇
▶ 속담 Never put off till tomorrow what you can do today
오늘 할 수 있는 것을 내일로 미루지 말라
▶ 속담 You get what you pay for 네가 값을 치른 것을 너는 얻는다

🎵 **노래 배우기(REmind)**

아래와 같이 앞서 배웠던 단어나 문구의 뜻을 말해보고 각자 문장을 만들어 보세요!!

Give thanks with a grateful heart

Give thanks *감사드리자*
with *~을 가지고, ~와 함께* ▶ with water *물을 가지고* ▶ with me *나와 함께*
grateful(=thankful, glad) *감사하는, 기쁜*
heart *마음, 심장*

Give thanks to the Holy One

thanks to ~ _____
holy _____ ▶ silent night holy night _____
  ▶ holiness _____
one _____

Give thanks because He's given Jesus Christ, His Son

because _____
He's given(= He has given) _____
give _____
Jesus Christ _____
His _____ ▶ His Son(=Jesus Christ) _____

And now let the weak say, "I am strong"

and _____ ↔ but _____
now _____ ▶ past _____ ▶ future _____
let _____ ▶ let me drink water _____
weak _____ ▶ the weak _____
say _____
strong _____ ▶ strength _____
  ▶ (PV) In unity, there is strength _____

Let the poor say, "I am rich"

poor _____ ▶ the poor _____
rich _____ ▶ the rich _____

Because of what the Lord has done for us

because of _____ ▶ because _____
what _____
  ▶ (PV) Never put _____ till tomorrow what you can do today

영한번역

Give thanks with a grateful heart	감사드리세 감사하는(기쁜) 마음으로
Give thanks to the Holy One	감사드리세 거룩한 존재(분)께
Give thanks because He's given Jesus Christ, His Son	감사드리세 왜냐하면 하나님께서 그의 아들인 예수님을 주셨기 때문에
Give thanks with a grateful heart	감사드리세 감사하는(기쁜) 마음으로
Give thanks to the Holy One	감사드리세 거룩한 존재께
Give thanks because He's given Jesus Christ, His Son	감사드리세 왜냐하면 하나님께서 그의 아들인 예수님을 주셨기 때문에
(refrain)	(후렴)
And now let the weak say, "I am strong"	그리고 이제는 약한 사람들이 '나는 강하다'라고 말할 수 있게 하시고,
Let the poor say, "I am rich"	가난한 사람들이 '나는 부유하다'라고 말할 수 있게 하시네
Because of what the Lord has done for us	왜냐하면 주님이 우리를 위해 하신 일 때문에
refrain	후렴
Give thanks with a grateful heart	감사드리세 감사하는(기쁜) 마음으로
Give thanks to the Holy One	감사드리세 거룩한 존재(분)께
Give thanks because He's given Jesus Christ, His Son	감사드리세 왜냐하면 하나님께서 그의 아들인 예수님을 주셨기 때문에
Give thanks with a grateful heart	감사드리세 감사하는(기쁜) 마음으로
Give thanks to the Holy One	감사드리세 거룩한 존재(분)께
Give thanks because He's given Jesus Christ, His Son	감사드리세 왜냐하면 하나님께서 그의 아들인 예수님을 주셨기 때문에
refrain	후렴
refrain	후렴
Give thanks	감사드리세
We Give thanks	우리 감사드리세
We Give thanks	우리 감사드리세

* 상기 번역은 영어공부를 위한 해석(직역)이며 공인된 한글 번역곡(가사)은 아님을 알려드립니다

번역해보기

Give thanks with a grateful heart
Give thanks to the Holy One
Give thanks because He's given Jesus Christ,
His Son

감사드리세 감사하는(기쁜) 마음으로

Give thanks with a grateful heart
Give thanks to the Holy One
Give thanks because He's given Jesus Christ,
His Son

(refrain)
And now let the weak say, "I am strong"

(후렴)
그리고 이제는 약한 사람들이 '나는 강하다'라고
말할 수 있게 하시고

Let the poor say, "I am rich"

Because of what the Lord has done for us

refrain
Give thanks with a grateful heart
Give thanks to the Holy One
Give thanks because He's given Jesus Christ,
His Son

Give thanks with a grateful heart
Give thanks to the Holy One
Give thanks because He's given Jesus Christ,
His Son

refrain
refrain
Give thanks
We Give thanks
We Give thanks

✚ 노래와 관련된 성경 말씀

앞서 배운 영어찬양과 관련된 성경말씀을 알아봅시다!!

For you know the grace of our Lord Jesus Christ, that though he was rich, yet for your sake he became poor, so that you through his poverty might become rich. (2 Corinthians 8:9)

우리 주 예수 그리스도의 은혜를 너희가 알거니와 부요하신 이로서 너희를 위하여 가난하게 되심은 그의 가난함으로 말미암아 너희를 부요하게 하려 하심이라. (고린도후서 8:9)

We give thanks to you, O God, we give thanks, for your Name is near; men tell of your wonderful deeds. (Psalm 75:1)

하나님이여 우리가 주께 감사하고 감사함은 주의 이름이 가까움이라 사람들이 주의 기이한 일들을 전파하나이다. (시편 75:1)

Let us come before him with thanksgiving and extol him with music and song. (Psalm 95:2)

우리가 감사함으로 그 앞에 나아가며 시를 지어 즐거이 그를 노래하자. (시편 95:2)

Praise the LORD. Give thanks to the LORD, for he is good; his love endures forever. (Psalm 106:1)

할렐루야 여호와께 감사하라 그는 선하시며 그 인자하심이 영원함이로다. (시편 106:1)

You are my God, and I will give you thanks; you are my God, and I will exalt you.
Give thanks to the LORD, for he is good; his love endures forever. (Psalms 118:28~29)

주는 나의 하나님이시라 내가 주께 감사하리이다 주는 나의 하나님이시라 내가 주를 높이리이다
여호와께 감사하라 그는 선하시며 그의 인자하심이 영원함이로다. (시편 118:28~29)

Be joyful always; pray continually; give thanks in all circumstances, for this is God's will for you in Christ Jesus. (1 Thessalonians 5:16~18)

항상 기뻐하라; 쉬지 말고 기도하라; 범사에 감사하라 이것이 그리스도 예수 안에서 너희를 향하신 하나님의 뜻이니라. (데살로니가전서 5:16~18)

But we ought always to thank God for you, brothers and sisters loved by the Lord, because God chose you as firstfruits to be saved through the sanctifying work of the Spirit and through belief in the truth. (2 Thessalonians 2:13)

주께서 사랑하시는 형제들아 우리가 항상 너희에 관하여 마땅히 하나님께 감사할 것은 하나님이 처음부터 너희를 택하사 성령의 거룩하게 하심과 진리를 믿음으로 구원을 받게 하심이니. (데살로니가후서 2:13)

"For God so loved the world that he gave his one and only Son, that whoever believes in him shall not perish but have eternal life. (John 3:16)

하나님이 세상을 이처럼 사랑하사 독생자를 주셨으니 이는 그를 믿는 자마다 멸망하지 않고 영생을 얻게 하려 하심이라. (요한복음 3:16)

Speak to one another with psalms, hymns and spiritual songs. Sing and make music in your heart to the Lord, always giving thanks to God the Father for everything, in the name of our Lord Jesus Christ. (Ephesians 5:19~20)

시와 찬송과 신령한 노래들로 서로 화답하며 너희의 마음으로 주께 노래하며 찬송하며
범사에 우리 주 예수 그리스도의 이름으로 항상 아버지 하나님께 감사하며 (에베소서 5:19~20)

(2 Corinthians 8:9) **for your shake** 당신을 위해 / for my shake 나를 위해 / for his sake 그를 위해
(Psalm 75:1) **deed** 행위 / do 행동하다
(Psalm 95:2) **extol** 칭송하다, 격찬하다 > praise 찬양하다, 칭찬하다
(1 Thessalonians 5:18) **circumstance** 상황, 환경, 처지
(2 Thessalonians 2:13) **ought to :** ~ 해야 한다

영어성경 말씀을 한글로 해석해 보기

앞서 배운 성경말씀을 소리 내어 읽어보고 해석해 보세요!!

For you know the grace of our Lord Jesus Christ, that though he was rich, yet for your sake he became poor, so that you through his poverty might become rich. (2 Corinthians 8:9)

We give thanks to you, O God, we give thanks, for your Name is near; men tell of your wonderful deeds. (Psalm 75:1)

Let us come before him with thanksgiving and extol him with music and song. (Psalm 95:2)

Praise the LORD. Give thanks to the LORD, for he is good; his love endures forever. (Psalm 106:1)

You are my God, and I will give you thanks; you are my God, and I will exalt you.
Give thanks to the LORD, for he is good; his love endures forever. (Psalms 118:28~29)

Be joyful always; pray continually; give thanks in all circumstances, for this is God's will for you in Christ Jesus. (1 Thessalonians 5:16~18)

But <u>we ought always to thank God</u> for you, brothers and sisters loved by the Lord, because God chose you as firstfruits to be saved through the sanctifying work of the Spirit and through belief in the truth. (2 Thessalonians 2:13)

"For <u>God so loved the world that he gave his one and only Son</u>, that whoever believes in him shall not perish but have eternal life. (John 3:16)

Speak to one another with psalms, hymns and spiritual songs. Sing and make music in your heart to the Lord,
<u>always giving thanks to God the Father for everything</u>, in the name of our Lord Jesus Christ.
(Ephesians 5:19~20)

Puzzle 2

✿ 'GIVE THANKS' 에서 배웠던 단어들로 퍼즐을 완성해 봅시다!

Across_가로	Down_세로
2 ~을 가지고, ~와 함께	**1** 미래
4 마음, 심장	**3** 감사하는, 고마워하는, 기쁜
7 강한, 힘센	**4** 거룩한
8 말하다	**5** 과거
9 부유한 ↔ poor	**6** 가난한 ↔ rich
	10 노래

정답은 책의 뒤편에서 확인하세요

3rd

God will make a way*

(refrain) God will make a way
Where there seems to be no way
He works in ways we cannot see
He will make a way for me
He will be my guide
Hold me closely to His side
With love and strength for each new day
He will make a way
He will make a way

------ refrain ------

By a roadway in the wilderness
He'll lead me
Rivers in the desert will I see
Heaven and Earth will fade

But His Word will still remain
And He will do something new today

------ refrain ------

By a roadway in the wilderness
He'll lead me
Rivers in the desert will I see
Heaven and Earth will fade
But His Word will still remain
And He will do something new today

------ refrain ------

With love and strength for each new day
He will make a way, He will make a way

◇ QR코드를 스캔하여 유튜브로 들어보세요!!
◇ 유튜브(www.youtube.com) 검색창에 아래와 같이 입력하고 돋보기를
클릭해도 됩니다.

God will make a way don moen   🔍

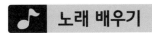 노래 알아보기

이곡은 2003년도에 발표된 "The Best of Don Moen"이란 앨범에 수록된 곡이며 1992년도 미국의 CCM(contemporary christian music) 음악상인 도브 어워드(Dove award)에서 올해의 노래로 선정된 바 있습니다. 우리나라에서는 '나의 가는 길'로 번안되어 불리고 있습니다.

이 노래는 돈모엔(Don Moen, 1950~) 목사님이 작곡하셨습니다. 돈모엔 목사님은 어느 날 아내의 여동생과 그녀의 남편 그리고 그들의 네 자녀가 타고 가던 차가 큰 트럭과 부딪혀 심한 교통사고를 당했고 그중 한 명의 자녀를 잃게 되었다는 소식을 듣게 되었습니다. 돈 모엔 목사님은 크게 상심해 있는 여동생과 그녀의 남편을 어떻게 위로해 주어야 할지 고민하며 하나님께 깊이 기도하던 중 이사야 43장 2절의 말씀을 받아 이 곡을 작곡 했다고 합니다. 돈 모엔 목사님은 우리가 어떤 고난을 겪더라도 하나님은 결코 우리를 잊지 않고 계시며 하나님께서 우리를 당신의 손바닥에 새기셨다는 하나님의 말씀을 이 노래를 통해 고백하십니다.

세상을 살다 보면 어떤 일이 왜 일어나는지 알 수 없는 경우가 많습니다. 그러나 지극하신 선이신 하나님은 우리가 알 수 없는 방법으로 가장 좋은 길을 예비하십니다. 어떤 상황 속에서도 가장 좋은 때에 가장 좋은 것으로 예비해 주실 하나님을 생각하며 이 노래를 배워봅시다.

♪ 노래 배우기

(refrain) God will make a way

> **refrain** 후렴
> **God** 하나님
> **will make** 만들 것이다
> **a** 어떤(some, certain), 하나의(one), 같은(same)
> **way** 길(road, path), 방법 또는 방식(method)

Where there seems to be no way

> **where** ~ ~에서
> **there seems to be** ~ ~처럼 보이다
> **Where there seems to be** ~ ~처럼 보이는 곳에서

He works in ways that we cannot see

> **work** 일하다
> **in ways** 방법들로, 방식들로 ▶ in many ways 여러모로
> **we** 우리 > I 나

cannot 불가능한 ↔ can 가능한
see 보다(see-saw-seen)
in ways that we cannot see 여기서 that은 접속사로서 that 뒤의 문장인 'we cannot see'는 'ways'를 꾸며주고 있습니다.

He will make a way for me

He 그, 여기서는 하나님(GOD)
will make 만드실 것이다
for me 나를 위하여

He will be my guide

my guide 나의 인도자 ▶ travel guide 여행 인도자 ▶ guidance 인도

Hold me closely to His side

hold 붙들다 ▶ **uphold** 지지하다
(He) **hold me** 그는 나를 붙드신다, 여기서는 He가 앞에 생략되어 있습니다
closely 가까이 ▶ **close** 가까운 ↔ far 먼
to His side 그(하나님)의 편으로

With love and strength for each new day

'with + 사람'은 '사람과 함께'로, 'with + 물건'은 '물건을 가지고'로 해석합니다
strength 힘 ▶ **strong** 힘센
with love and strength 사랑과 힘으로
each 각각의 ▶ **each time** 매번 ▶ **each day** 매일
new 새로운 ↔ **old** 오래된
속담 Don't put new wine into old bottle. 새 포도주를 오래된 병에 담지 말라

He will make a way, He will make a way

By a roadway in the wilderness, He'll lead me

roadway 길가, 차도 ▶ by the roadway 도로 옆에
wilderness 광야, 황무지, 불모지
lead (lead-led-led) 이끌다 ▶ **leader** 이끄는 사람, 지도자

Rivers in the desert will I see

river 강 < **sea** 바다
desert[데~저트] 사막 ▶ **dessert**[디저~트] 후식
rivers in the desert will I see = I will see rivers in the desert

Heaven and earth will fade

heaven 하늘, 천국 ↔ **earth** 땅, 지구
fade 서서히 사라지다, 희미해지다, (명사로는) 도망
▶ **fade in** 점점 또렷해지며 나타남 ↔ **fade out** 점점 희미해지며 사라짐
▶ 속담 All that's fair must fade 아름다운 것은 모두 반드시 시들기 마련이다

But His Word will still remain

word 말, 여기서는 대문자로 시작하여 '하나님의 말씀'이라는 의미임
still 아직도, 계속, 가만히
remain 남다 ▶ **remnant** 나머지 ▶ **righteous remnant** 남은 의인

He will do something new today.

something 어떤 것, 중요한 것 ↔ **nothing** 아무것도 아닌 것
today 오늘 ▶ **yesterday** 어제 ▶ **tomorrow** 내일
▶ 속담 Never put off till tomorrow what you can do today
오늘 할 수 있는 것을 내일로 미루지 마라

 노래 배우기(REmind)

아래와 같이 앞서 배웠던 단어나 문구의 뜻을 말해보고 각자 문장을 만들어 보세요!!

(refrain) God will make a way

refrain _후렴_
God _하나님_
will make _만들 것이다_
a _어떤_ (some, certain), _하나의_ (one), _같은_ (same)
way _길_ (road, path), _방법, 방식_ (method)

Where there seems to be no way

where ~ ....
there seems to be ~ ....
Where there seems to be ~ ....

He works in ways that we cannot see

work ....
in ways .... ▶ **in many ways** ....
we .... > **i** ....

cannot _____ ↔ can _____
see _____ (see- _____ - _____)

He will make a way for me

He _____ ↔ she _____
will make _____
for me _____

He will be my guide

my guide _____ ▶ travel guide _____ ▶ guidance _____

Hold me closely to His side

hold _____ ▶ uphold _____
closely _____ ▶ close _____ ↔ far _____
to His side _____

With love and strength for each new day

strength _____ ▶ strong _____
with love and strength _____
each _____
new _____ ↔ old _____
속담 Don't put new wine into old bottle _____

He will make a way, He will make a way

By a roadway in the wilderness, He'll lead me

roadway _____ ▶ by the roadway _____
wilderness _____
lead _____ (lead - _____ - _____) ▶ leader _____

Rivers in the desert will I see

river _____ < sea _____
desert _____ ▶ dessert _____

Heaven and earth will fade

heaven _____ ↔ earth _____
fade _____
▶ **fade in** _____ ↔ **fade out** _____
▶ 속담 All that is _____ must fade

But His Word will still remain

word _____
still _____
remain _____ ▶ **remnant** _____ ▶ **righteous remnant** _____

He will do something new today

something _____ ↔ **nothing** _____
today _____ ▶ **yesterday** _____ ▶ **tomorrow** _____
▶ 속담 Never put off till tomorrow _____ you can do today

(refrain) God will make a way	(후렴) 하나님은 길을 만드실 것이네
Where there seems to be no way	길이 없어 보이는 곳에
He works in ways that we cannot see	그는 우리가 볼 수 없는 방법으로 일하시네
He will make a way for me	그는 나를 위해 길을 만드실 것이네
He will be my guide	그는 나의 인도자가 되실 것이네
Hold me closely to His side	그의 편으로 가까이 나를 붙드시네
With love and strength for each new day	사랑과 힘으로 매일 새로운 날마다
He will make a way, He will make a way	그는 길을 만드실 것이네, 그는 길을 만드실 것이네
refrain	후렴
By a roadway in the wilderness, He'll lead me	광야의 길가에서, 그는 나를 이끄실 것이네
Rivers in the desert will I see	사막에서 강을 나는 볼 것이네
Heaven and earth will fade	하늘과 땅은 닳아 없어질 것이다
But His Word will still remain	그러나 그의 말씀은 계속 남아있으리
He will do something new today	그는 오늘 새로운 일을 행하시리
refrain	후렴
By a roadway in the wilderness, He'll lead me	광야의 길가에서, 그는 나를 이끄실 것이네
Rivers in the desert will I see	사막에서 강을 나는 볼 것이네
Heaven and earth will fade	하늘과 땅은 닳아 없어질 것이다
But His Word will still remain	그러나 그의 말씀은 계속 남아있으리
He will do something new today	그는 오늘 새로운 일을 행하시리
refrain	후렴
With love and strength for each new day	사랑과 힘으로 매일 새로운 날마다
He will make a way, He will make a way	그는 길을 만드실 것이네, 그는 길을 만드실 것이네

* 상기 번역은 영어공부를 위한 해석(직역)이며 공인된 한글 번역곡(가사)은 아님을 알려드립니다

번역해보기

(refrain) God will make a way

Where there seems to be no way

He works in ways that we cannot see

He will make a way for me

He will be my guide

Hold me closely to His side

With love and strength for each new day

He will make a way, He will make a way

refrain

By a roadway in the wilderness, He'll lead me

Rivers in the desert will I see

Heaven and earth will fade

But His Word will still remain

He will do something new today

refrain

By a roadway in the wilderness, He'll lead me

Rivers in the desert will I see

Heaven and earth will fade

But His Word will still remain

He will do something new today

refrain

With love and strength for each new day

He will make a way, He will make a way

(후렴) 하나님은 길을 만드실 것이네

광야의 길에서, 그는 나를 이끄실 것이네

✚ 노래와 관련된 성경 말씀

앞서 배운 영어찬양과 관련된 성경말씀을 알아봅시다!!

When you pass through the waters, I will be with you; and when you pass through the rivers, they will not sweep over you. When you walk through the fire, you will not be burned; the flames will not set you ablaze (Isaiah 43:2)

네가 물 가운데로 지날 때에 내가 함께 할 것이라 강을 건널 때에 물이 너를 침몰하지 못할 것이며 네가 불 가운데로 지날 때에 타지도 아니할 것이요 불꽃이 너를 사르지도 못하리니 (이사야 43:2)

"Forget the former things; do not dwell on the past.
See, I am doing a new thing! Now it springs up; do you not perceive it? I am making a way in the desert and streams in the wasteland. (Isaiah 43:18~19)

너희는 이전 일을 기억하지 말며 옛날 일을 생각하지 말라
보라 내가 새 일을 행하리니 이제 나타낼 것이라 너희가 그것을 알지 못하겠느냐 반드시 내가 광야에 길을 사막에 강을 내리니. (이사야 43:18~19)

Can a mother forget the baby at her breast and have no compassion on the child she has borne? Though she may forget, I will not forget you! See, I have engraved you on the palms of my hands; your walls are ever before me (Isaiah 49:15~16)

여인이 어찌 그 젖 먹는 자식을 잊겠으며 자기 태에서 난 아들을 긍휼히 여기지 않겠느냐 그들은 혹시 잊을지라도 나는 너를 잊지 아니할 것이라 내가 너를 내 손바닥에 새겼고 너의 성벽이 항상 내 앞에 있나니 (이사야 49:15~16)

Surely he took up our infirmities and carried our sorrows, yet we considered him stricken by God, smitten by him, and afflicted.
But he was pierced for our transgressions, he was crushed for our iniquities; the punishment that brought us peace was upon him, and by his wounds we are healed.
We all, like sheep, have gone astray, each of us has turned to his own way; and the LORD has laid on him the iniquity of us all. (Isaiah 53:4~6)

그는 실로 우리의 질고를 지고 우리의 슬픔을 당하였거늘 우리는 생각하기를 그는 징벌을 받아 하나님께 맞으며 고난을 당한다 하였노라 그가 찔림은 우리의 허물 때문이요
그가 상함은 우리의 죄악 때문이라 그가 징계를 받으므로 우리는 평화를 누리고 그가 채찍에 맞으므로 우리는 나음을 받았도다
우리는 다 양 같아서 그릇 행하여 각기 제 길로 갔거늘 여호와께서는 우리 모두의 죄악을 그에게 담당시키셨도다.
(이사야 53:4~6)

I know, O LORD, that a man's life is not his own; it is not for man to direct his steps. (Jeremiah 10:23)

여호와여 내가 알거니와 사람의 길이 자신에게 있지 아니하니 걸음을 지도함이 걷는 자에게 있지 아니하니이다. (예레미야 10:23)

But he knows the way that I take; when he has tested me, I will come forth as gold. (Job 23:10)

그러나 내가 가는 길을 그가 아시나니 그가 나를 단련하신 후에는 내가 순금 같이 되어 나오리라. (욥기 23:10)

Trust in the LORD with all your heart and lean not on your own understanding; in all your ways acknowledge him, and he will make your paths straight. (proverbs 3:5~6)

너는 마음을 다하여 여호와를 신뢰하고 네 명철을 의지하지 말라
너는 범사에 그를 인정하라 그리하면 네 길을 지도하시리라. (잠언 3:5~6)

The LORD himself goes before you and will be with you; he will never leave you nor forsake you. Do not be afraid; do not be discouraged." (Deuteronomy 31:8)

그리하면 여호와 그가 네 앞에서 가시며 너와 함께 하사 너를 떠나지 아니하시며 버리지 아니하시리니 너는 두려워하지 말라 놀라지 말라. (신명기 31:8)

Heaven and earth will pass away, but my words will never pass away. (Matthew 24:35)

천지는 없어질지언정 내 말은 없어지지 아니하리라 (마태복음 24:35)

For, "All men are like grass, and all their glory is like the flowers of the field; the grass withers and the flowers fall, but the word of the Lord stands forever." And this is the word that was preached to you. (1 peter 1:24~25)

그러므로 모든 육체는 풀과 같고 그 모든 영광은 풀의 꽃과 같으니 풀은 마르고 꽃은 떨어지되
오직 주의 말씀은 세세토록 있도다 하였으니 너희에게 전한 복음이 곧 이 말씀이니라 (베드로전서 1:24~25)

(Isaiah 43:2) **sweep** (빗자루 등으로) 쓸다, 휩쓸다 / **ablaze** 화염에 싸여서, 타오르는
(Isaiah 53:6) **go(get) astray** 길을 잃다, 정도를 벗어나다(타락하다)
　　　　　　　iniquity 부정, 불법 / **inequity** 불공평, 불공정
(Job 23:10) **forth**(= forward) 앞으로, 밖으로
(proverbs 3:5) **lean on** ~에 의지하다, 기대다
(Matthew 24:35) **pass away** 사망하다, 사라지다
(1 peter 1:24) **wither** 시들다, 쇠약해지다, 시들게 하다, 쇠약해지게 하다
(1 peter 1:25) **preach** 전도하다, 설교하다

영어성경 말씀을 한글로 해석해 보기

앞서 배운 성경말씀을 소리 내어 읽어보고 해석해 보세요!!

When you pass through the waters, I will be with you; and when you pass through the rivers, they will not sweep over you. When you walk through the fire, you will not be burned; the flames will not set you ablaze (Isaiah 43:2)

"Forget the former things; do not dwell on the past.
See, I am doing a new thing! Now it springs up; do you not perceive it? I am making a way in the desert and streams in the wasteland. (Isaiah 43:18~19)

Can a mother forget the baby at her breast and have no compassion on the child she has borne? Though she may forget, I will not forget you!
See, I have engraved you on the palms of my hands; your walls are ever before me
(Isaiah 49:15~16)

Surely he took up our infirmities and carried our sorrows, yet we considered him stricken by God, smitten by him, and afflicted.
But he was pierced for our transgressions, he was crushed for our iniquities; the punishment that brought us peace was upon him, and by his wounds we are healed.
We all, like sheep, have gone astray, each of us has turned to his own way; and the LORD has laid on him the iniquity of us all. (Isaiah 53:4~6)

I know, O LORD, that a man's life is not his own; it is not for man to direct his steps. (Jeremiah 10:23)

But he knows the way that I take; when he has tested me, I will come forth as gold. (Job 23:10)

Trust in the LORD with all your heart and lean not on your own understanding; in all your ways acknowledge him, and he will make your paths straight. (proverbs 3:5~6)

The LORD himself goes before you and will be with you; he will never leave you nor forsake you. Do not be afraid; do not be discouraged." (Deuteronomy 31:8)

Heaven and earth will pass away, but my words will never pass away. (Matthew 24:35)

For, "All men are like grass, and all their glory is like the flowers of the field; the grass withers and the flowers fall, but the word of the Lord stands forever." And this is the word that was preached to you. (1 peter 1:24~25)

Puzzle 3

🚩 'GOD WILL MAKE A WAY' 에서 배웠던 단어들로 퍼즐을 완성해 봅시다!

Across_가로	Down_세로
2 인도자, Travel	**1** 이끄는 사람, 지도자
4 땅, 지구	**3** 사막
7 어제	**5** 길 (= road, path)
8 힘, 형용사는 strong	**6** 일, 일하다
10 오늘	**9** 하늘, 천국
11 병, 술병	
▶ Don't put new wine into old _____	
12 새로운 ↔ old	

정답은 책의 뒤편에서 확인하세요

MEMO

4th
God is the strength of my heart*

(refrain) God is the strength of my heart
God is the strength of my heart
God is the strength of my heart
and my portion forever, forever

------- refrain -------

Whom have I in heaven but You
There is nothing on earth I desire besides You
My heart and my strength
many times they fail
But there is one truth
that always will prevail

------- refrain × 7 -------

Forever, forever

◇ QR코드를 스캔하여 유튜브로 들어보세요!!
◇ 유튜브(www.youtube.com) 검색창에 아래와 같이 입력하고 돋보기를
   클릭해도 됩니다.

| God is the strength of my heart don moen | 🔍 |

노래 알아보기

이곡은 'purify my heart'로 유명한 예배 인도자인 유진 그레코(Eugene Greco)가 작곡한 곡입니다. 1993년 호산나 뮤직(Hosanna Music)에서 발표된 앨범인 "Praise & Worship - Mighty God"에 수록되었으며, 돈 모엔(Don Moen) 목사님이 버지니아주의 리버티 대학에서 7,000명의 찬양단과 함께 녹음하여 1998년 발표한 앨범인 'God is Good'에도 수록되어 있습니다. 한국에서는 '하늘위에 주님밖에'라는 이름으로 번안되어 여러 찬양그룹에 의해 불리고 있습니다. 우리나라 찬양그룹인 마커스(MARKERS)와 제이어스(J-US)가 부른 이 찬양을 들어보면 영어버전처럼 역시 주님의 힘과 능력을 느껴집니다.

 노래 배우기

(refrain) God is the strength of my heart

> **refrain** 후렴
> **God** 하나님
> **strength** 힘 ▶ **strong** 힘센 ↔ weak 약한
> **heart** 마음, 심장, 가슴

God is the strength of my heart
God is the strength of my heart
and my portion forever, forever

> **my** 나의
> **portion** (분배받은) 몫, 분깃, 부분, 물약
> **forever** 영원히

refrain

Whom have I in heaven but You

> **whom** 누군가, 누군가를, who를 목적어(~를) 자리에 쓸 때 사용하는 말
> **heaven** 하늘, 천국 ↔ earth 땅, 지구
> ▶ 속담 Heaven helps those who help themselves. (하늘은 스스로 돕는 자들을 돕는다.)
> but 일반적으로 '그러나'라는 의미로 쓰이나, '제외하고'라는 의미로도 많이 사용되며 여기서는 '제외하고(except)'라는 의미입니다.
> but You = except You 당신을 제외하고는, 하나님 외에는

There is nothing on earth I desire besides You

There is ~ ~가 있다
nothing 아무것도 아닌 것 ↔ **something** 중요한 것
on ~ 위에 ▶ on the table 탁자 위에
desire 정말로(간절히) 원하다 > want 원하다
besides (부정문 또는 의문문에서) ~을 제외하고는 = except
besides You = except You = but You 당신을 제외하고는, 하나님 외에는

My heart and my strength

heart 마음, 심장, 가슴 ▶ He has a kind heart 그는 친절한 마음을 가지고 있다
strength 힘 ▶ strong 힘센

many times they fail

many 많은
times 때, 시간, 세월
속담 A stitch in times saves nine 적당한 때 한 땀이 아홉 땀의 수고를 덜어준다 (= There is a time for everything)
속담 Time files like an arrow 세월은 화살과 같이 날아간다
they 그들, 여기서는 'My heart and my strength'
fail 실패하다 ↔ succeed 성공하다 ▶ failure 실패 ↔ success 성공

But there is one truth

truth 진실, 진리 ↔ falsehood 거짓
▶ true 진짜인, 사실인 ↔ false 가짜인, 거짓된

that always will prevail

always 항상 = all the way
will ~ 할 것이다
prevail 우세하다, 승리하다, 널리퍼지다
▶ prevail against(over) Satan 사탄에게 승리하다

refrain ×7

Forever, forever

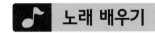 노래 배우기

아래와 같이 앞서 배웠던 단어나 문구의 뜻을 말해보고 각자 문장을 만들어 보세요!!

(refrain) God is the strength of my heart

God *하나님*
strength *힘* ▶ strong *힘쎈* ↔ weak *약한*
heart *마음, 심장, 가슴*

God is the strength of my heart
God is the strength of my heart
and my portion forever, forever

my
portion
forever

refrain
Whom have I in heaven but You

whom
heaven   ↔ **earth**
▶ 속담 Heaven helps those who help
but   ▶ but You =   You

There is nothing on earth I desire besides You

There is
nothing   ↔ something
on ~   ▶ on the table
desire   > want
beside You

My heart and my strength

heart   ▶ He has a kind heart
strength   ▶ strong

many times they fail

many _____
time _____
- 속담 A stitch in times _____ nine
- 속담 Time _____ like an arrow
fail _____ ↔ succeed _____ ▶ failure

But there is one truth

truth _____ ↔ _____
▶ **true** _____ ↔ **false** _____

that always will prevail

always(= all the way) _____
will ~ _____
prevail _____ ▶ prevail against(_____) Satan
▶ prevail against bad habits _____

refrain ✕7

Forever, forever

영한번역

(refrain)

God is the strength of my heart

God is the strength of my heart

God is the strength of my heart

and my portion forever, forever

(후렴)

하나님은 나의 마음의 힘입니다

하나님은 나의 마음의 힘입니다

하나님은 나의 마음의 힘입니다

그리고 나의 몫입니다 영원히, 영원히

refrain

후렴

Whom have I in heaven but You

There is nothing on earth I desire besides
You

My heart and my strength

many times they fail

But there is one truth

that always will prevail

하늘에서 당신(하나님) 외에 누가 나에게
있습니까

당신과 비교하여 내가 세상에서 간절히
원하는 것은 아무것도 없습니다.

나의 마음 그리고 나의 힘

그들은 자주 실패합니다.

그러나 항상 승리하는

하나의 진리가 있습니다

refrain ×7

후렴 ×7

Forever, forever

영원히, 영원히

* 상기 번역은 영어공부를 위한 해석(직역)이며 공인된 한글 번역곡(가사)은 아님을 알려드립니다

번역해보기

(refrain)

God is the strength of my heart

God is the strength of my heart

God is the strength of my heart

and my portion forever, forever

(후렴)

하나님은 나의 마음의 힘입니다

refrain

Whom have I in heaven but You

There is nothing on earth I desire besides

You

My heart and my strength

many times they fail

But there is one truth

that always will prevail

하늘에서 당신(하나님)외에 누가 나에게 있습니까

refrain ×7

Forever, forever

✝ 노래와 관련된 성경 말씀

앞서 배운 영어찬양과 관련된 성경말씀을 알아봅시다!!

The LORD is my strength and my song; he has become my salvation. He is my God, and I will praise him, my father's God, and I will exalt him. (Exodus 15:2)

여호와는 나의 힘이요 노래시며 나의 구원이시로다 그는 나의 하나님이시니 내가 그를 찬송할 것이요 내 아버지의 하나님이시니 내가 그를 높이리로다. (출애굽기 15:2)

Look to the LORD and his strength; seek his face always. (1 Chronicles 16:11)

여호와와 그의 능력을 구할지어다 항상 그의 얼굴을 찾을지어다. (연대기상 16:11)

but those who hope in the LORD will renew their strength. They will soar on wings like eagles; they will run and not grow weary, they will walk and not be faint. (Isaiah 40:31)

오직 여호와를 앙망하는 자는 새 힘을 얻으리니 독수리 날개치며 올라감 같을 것이요 달음박질 하여도 곤비치 아니하겠고 걸어가도 피곤치 아니하리로다 (이사야 40장31절)

So do not fear, for I am with you; do not be dismayed, for I am your God. I will strengthen you and help you; I will uphold you with my righteous right hand. (Isaiah 41:10)

두려워 말라 내가 너와 함께 함이니라 놀라지 마라 나는 네 하나님이 됨이니라 내가 너를 굳세게 하리라 참으로 너를 도와 주리라 참으로 나의 의로운 오른손으로 너를 붙들리라. (이사야 41장10절)

The LORD is my strength and my shield; my heart trusts in him, and he helps me. My heart leaps for joy, and with my song I praise him. (Psalm 28:7)

여호와는 나의 힘과 나의 방패이시니 내 마음이 그를 의지하여 도움을 얻었도다 그러므로 내 마음이 크게 기뻐하며 내 노래로 그를 찬송하리로다 (시편 28:7)

For who is God besides the LORD? And who is the Rock except our God?

It is God who arms me with strength and makes my way perfect. (Psalm 18:31~32)

여호와 외에 누가 하나님이며 우리 하나님 외에 누가 반석이냐

이 하나님이 힘으로 내게 띠 띠우시며 내 길을 완전하게 하시며 (시편 18:31~32)

Whom have I in heaven but you? And there is nothing on earth that I desire besides you.

(Psalm 73:25, ESV)

하늘에서는 주 외에 누가 내게 있으리요 땅에서는 주 밖에 내가 사모할 이 없나이다 (시편 73:25)

My flesh and my heart may fail, but God is the strength of my heart and my portion forever.

(Psalm 73:26)

내 육체와 마음은 쇠잔하나 하나님은 내 마음의 반석이시요 영원한 분깃이라 (시편 73:26)

I can do all this through him who gives me strength. (Philippians 4:13)

내게 능력(힘) 주시는 자 안에서 내가 모든 것을 할 수 있느니라 (빌립보서 4:13)

(Isaiah 40:31) **soar** 높이 날아오르다, 급상승하다
faint 약한(=weak), 어렴풋한, 희미한
(Isaiah 41:10) **dismay** 당황하다, 낙담하다, 실망하다
(Psalm 18:32) **arm** A **with** B A를 B로 무장시키다

🔊 영어성경 말씀을 한글로 해석해 보기

앞서 배운 성경말씀을 소리 내어 읽어보고 해석해 보세요!!

The LORD is my strength and my song; he has become my salvation. He is my God, and I will praise him, my father's God, and I will exalt him. (Exodus 15:2)

Look to the LORD and his strength; seek his face always. (1 Chronicles 16:11)

but those who hope in the LORD will renew their strength. They will soar on wings like eagles; they will run and not grow weary, they will walk and not be faint. (Isaiah 40:31)

So do not fear, for I am with you; do not be dismayed, for I am your God. I will strengthen you and help you; I will uphold you with my righteous right hand. (Isaiah 41:10)

The LORD is my strength and my shield; my heart trusts in him, and he helps me. My heart leaps for joy, and with my song I praise him. (Psalm 28:7)

For who is God besides the LORD? And who is the Rock except our God?
It is God who arms me with strength and makes my way perfect. (Psalm 18:31~32)

My flesh and my heart may fail, but God is the strength of my heart and my portion forever. (Psalm 73:26)

I can do all this through him who gives me strength. (Philippians 4:13)

Puzzle 4

'GOD IS THE STRENGTH OF MY HEART' 에서 배웠던 단어들로 퍼즐을 완성해 봅시다!

Across_가로	Down_세로
3 영원히	**1** 우세하다, 승리하다, 널리퍼지다
5 화살	Truth will _____
6 진실, 진리 ↔ falsehood 거짓	**2** 정말로(간절히) 원하다 > want
8 날아가다, 파리	**4** 항상 (= all the way)
9 (분배받은) 몫, 분깃, 부분, 물약	**7** 마음, 심장, 가슴
	8 실패하다 ↔ succeed 성공하다
	10 제외하고(= besides)
	11 그러나

정답은 책의 뒤편에서 확인하세요

MEMO

If I come to Jesus

If I come to Jesus,
He will make me glad;
He will give me pleasure
When my heart is sad

(refrain) If I come to Jesus,
Happy I shall be
He is gently calling
Little ones like me

If I come to Jesus
He will hear my prayer;
He will love me dearly,
He my sins did bear

------- refrain -------

If I come to Jesus
He will take my hand,
He will kindly lead me
To a better land

------- refrain -------

◇ QR코드를 스캔하여 유튜브로 들어보세요!!

◇ 유튜브(www.youtube.com) 검색창에 아래와 같이 입력하고 돋보기를
클릭해도 됩니다.

 If I come to Jesus | 🔍

노래 알아보기

이곡은 평생을 시각장애인으로 살면서도 8,000편이 넘는 찬송시를 쓴 페니 크로스비(Fanny Crosby, 1820-1915) 여사의 찬송시를 바탕으로, 평생 2,000곡이 넘는 찬양곡을 작곡한 성공한 사업가이자 주일학교 음악 단장이었던 윌리엄 하워드 돈(William Howard Doane, 1832-1915)이 작곡한 찬송입니다. 이곡은 새찬송가 565장, '예수께로 가면'으로도 널리 알려져 있고 주일학교에서도 많이 부르고 있는 곡이기도 합니다. 크로스비 여사는 평생을 시각장애로 살았지만, 세상의 아름다움과 재미에 마음이 흔들리지 않고 하나님을 찬양하는 것에 더욱 집중할 수 있음에 감사하며 일생을 기쁨과 성령 충만함으로 살았습니다. 크로스비 여사가 95세를 사는 동안 열정적으로 쓴 8,000여 편의 찬송시를 통하여 고아, 과부, 맹인, 대통령 등을 포함한 각계각층의 사람들이 하나님의 사랑과 위로를 받았으며, 그녀의 찬송시는 많은 작곡가들에 의해 유명한 찬송가로 작곡되어 지금까지도 불리고 있습니다.

노래 배우기

If I come to Jesus,

If 만약 ~ 라면, 만일 ~ 이면 ↔ unless 만약 ~ 하지 않으면
come to ~ ~에게 (나아)가다

He will make me glad

make 만들다
glad 기쁜, 반가운 ▶ (I'm) glad to meet you 만나서 기뻐(반가워)!

He will give me pleasure

give 주다 ▶ give thanks 감사드리자
pleasure 기쁨(=joy)
▶ It's my pleasure 기꺼이 해드리죠(그렇게 하는 것은 나의 기쁨입니다)

When my heart is sad

When ~할 때
heart 마음, 가슴, 심장
sad 슬픈 ↔ happy 기쁜

If I come to Jesus,

Happy I shall be

Happy I shall be = I shall be happy

happy 즐거운 ↔ sad 슬픈

shall ~하게 되다

> 속담 As you sow, so shall you reap 뿌린 대로 거둘 것이다

> 속담 Ask, and it shall be given to you 구하라, 그러면 너에게 주어질 것이다

He is gently calling

gently 부드럽게(온화하게) ▶ **gentle** 부드러운(온화한) ▶ **gentleman** 신사

calling 부르고 있는, 소명, 직업 ▶ call 부르다

Little ones like me

little 작은 ↔ **big** 큰 ▶ **little one** 작은 이

like ~처럼, ~와 같이, 좋아하다 ▶ **like me** 나처럼

If I come to Jesus

He will hear my prayer

hear 듣다(hear-heard-heard)

prayer 기도 ▶ pray 기도하다

He will love me dearly

love 사랑하다 > **like** 좋아하다

dearly 매우, 대단히, 비싼 대가를 치르고 ▶ **dear** 사랑하는, 소중한

He my sins did bear

He my sins did bear(= He did bear my sins) 목적어(my sins)가 도치된 문장입니다

sin 죄, 죄악, 잘못 ▶ sinful 죄가 되는, 나쁜

bear 참다, 참아내다, 곰

> I can't bear the repeated sin 나는 반복되는 죄를 참을 수 없다

did bear 정말로 참아내다, do를 동사 앞에 쓰면 동사를 강조하는 의미인데 과거이므로 did를 썼습니다

refrain 후렴

refrain 후렴

If I come to Jesus

He will take my hand,

take (물건을)가지고 가다, (사람이나 동물을)데리고 가다 (take-took-taken)
hand 손, 도움 ▶ handful 한줌 ▶ handy 편리한, 손재주가 있는

He will kindly lead me

kindly 친절하게도 ▶ kind 친절한
lead 이끌다(lead-led-led) ▶ leader 인도자, 지도자

To a better land

better 더 좋은 ▶ good < better < the best
▶ 속담 Better late than never 늦는 것이 안 하는 것보다는 낫다
▶ 속담 Two hands are better than one. 두 개의 손이 한 개의 손 보다 낫다
land 땅 ▶ land of promise 약속의 땅

refrain 후렴

 노래 배우기(REmind)

아래와 같이 앞서 배웠던 단어나 문구의 뜻을 말해보고 각자 문장을 만들어 보세요!!

If I come to Jesus,

If *만약 ~ 라면, 만일 ~ 이면* ↔ **unless** *만약 ~ 하지 않으면*
come to *~ ~에게 (나아)가다*

He will make me glad

make _____

glad _____ ▶ (I'm) glad to meet you _____

He will give me pleasure

give _____ ▶ give thanks _____

pleasure(=joy) _____

▶ It's my pleasure _____

When my heart is sad

When _____

heart _____

sad _____ ↔ happy _____

If I come to Jesus,

Happy I shall be

Happy I shall be = I shall be

happy _____ ↔ sad _____

shall _____

▶ 속담 As you sow, so shall you _____

▶ 속담 _____ , and it shall be given to you

He is gently calling

gently _____ ▶ gentle _____ ▶ gentleman _____

calling _____ ▶ call _____

Little ones like me

little _____ ↔ big _____ ▶ little one _____

like _____ ▶ like me _____

If I come to Jesus

He will hear my prayer

hear _____ (hear- _____ - _____)

prayer _____ ▶ pray _____

He will love me dearly

love _____ > like _____

dearly _____ ▶ dear _____

He my sins did bear

He my sins did bear(= He did bear _____)

sin _____ ▶ **sinful** _____

bear _____ ▶ I can't bear the repeated sin

did bear _____

refrain × 2

If I come to Jesus

He will take my hand,

take _____ (take - took - _____)

hand _____ ▶ **handful** _____ ▶ **handy** _____

He will kindly lead me

kindly _____ ▶ **kind** _____

lead _____ (lead - _____ - led) ▶ **leader** _____

To a better land

better _____ ▶ **good** < _____ < **the best**

▶ 속담 Better _____ than never

▶ 속담 Two hands are better _____ one

land _____ ▶ land of promise _____

refrain

영한번역

If I come to Jesus,	내가 예수님께로 가면
He will make me glad;	그는 나를 기쁘게 해주실 것입니다
He will give me pleasure	그는 나에게 기쁨을 주실 것입니다
When my heart is sad.	내 마음이 슬플 때
(refrain) If I come to Jesus,	(후렴) 내가 예수님께로 가면
Happy I shall be.	나는 기쁠 것입니다
He is gently calling	그는 부드럽게 부르십니다
Little ones like me.	나와 같은 어린이들을
If I come to Jesus	내가 예수님께 나가면
He will hear my prayer;	예수님은 나의 기도를 들으실 것입니다
He will love me dearly,	예수님은 나를 매우 사랑해 주실 것입니다
He my sins did bear.	예수님은 나의 잘못을 정말로 참아주셨습니다
refrain	후렴
If I come to Jesus	내가 예수님께 나가면
He will take my hand,	예수님은 나의 손을 잡아주실 것입니다
He will kindly lead me	예수님은 나를 친절하게 이끌어 주십니다
To a better land.	더 좋은 곳으로
refrain	후렴

번역해보기

If I come to Jesus,

He will make me glad;

He will give me pleasure

When my heart is sad.

(refrain) If I come to Jesus,

Happy I shall be.

He is gently calling

Little ones like me.

If I come to Jesus

He will hear my prayer;

He will love me dearly,

He my sins did bear.

refrain

If I come to Jesus

He will take my hand,

He will kindly lead me

To a better land.

refrain

내가 예수님께로 가면

✟ 노래와 관련된 성경 말씀

앞서 배운 영어찬양과 관련된 성경말씀을 알아봅시다!!

The LORD your God is with you, he is mighty to save. He will take great delight in you, he will quiet you with his love, he will rejoice over you with singing." (Zephaniah 3:17)

너의 하나님 여호와가 너의 가운데에 계시니 그는 구원을 베푸실 전능자이시라 그가 너로 말미암아 기쁨을 이기지 못하시며 너를 잠잠히 사랑하시며 너로 말미암아 즐거이 부르며 기뻐하시리라 하리라 (스바냐 3:17)

People were also bringing babies to Jesus to have him touch them. When the disciples saw this, they rebuked them. But Jesus called the children to him and said, "Let the little children come to me, and do not hinder them, for the kingdom of God belongs to such as these. (Luke 18:15~16)

사람들이 예수께서 만져 주심을 바라고 자기 어린 아기를 데리고 오매 제자들이 보고 꾸짖거늘 예수께서 그 어린 아이들을 불러 가까이 하시고 이르시되 어린 아이들이 내게 오는 것을 용납하고 금하지 말라 하나님의 나라가 이런 자의 것이니라 (누가 18:15~16)

All that the Father gives me will come to me, and whoever comes to me I will never drive away (John 6:37)

아버지께서 내게 주시는 자는 다 내게로 올 것이요 내게 오는 자는 내가 결코 내쫓지 아니하리라 (요한복음 6:37)

On the last and greatest day of the Feast, Jesus stood and said in a loud voice, "If anyone is thirsty, let him come to me and drink
Whoever believes in me, as the Scripture has said, streams of living water will flow from within him." (John 7:37-38)

명절 끝날 곧 큰 날에 예수께서 서서 외쳐 이르시되 누구든지 목마르거든 내게로 와서 마시라
나를 믿는 자는 성경에 이름과 같이 그 배에서 생수의 강이 흘러나오리라 하시니 (요한복음 7:37-38)

(Luke 18:16) **hinder** 방해하다, 늦게 하다 / **belong to ~** ~에 속하다
(John 7:38) **stream** 흐름, 조류, 시냇물

영어성경 말씀을 한글로 해석해 보기

앞서 배운 성경말씀을 소리 내어 읽어보고 해석해 보세요!!

The LORD your God is with you, he is mighty to save. He will take great delight in you, he will quiet you with his love, he will rejoice over you with singing." (Zephaniah 3:17)

People were also bringing babies to Jesus to have him touch them. When the disciples saw this, they rebuked them.
But Jesus called the children to him and said, "Let the little children come to me, and do not hinder them, for the kingdom of God belongs to such as these. (Luke 18:15~16)

All that the Father gives me will come to me, and whoever comes to me I will never drive away (John 6:37)

On the last and greatest day of the Feast, Jesus stood and said in a loud voice, "If anyone is thirsty, let him come to me and drink
Whoever believes in me, as the Scripture has said, streams of living water will flow from within him." (John 7:37-38)

Puzzle 5

'IF I COME TO JESUS' 에서 배웠던 단어들로 퍼즐을 완성해 봅시다!

	Across_가로
2	더 좋은 > good
3	기쁜
7	수확하다, 거둬들이다
8	친절한
9	씨뿌리다
	▶ You reap what you _____
11	사랑, 사랑하다
12	슬픈

	Down_세로
1	기도
	▶ the Lord's _____ 주기도문
3	손, 도움
4	기쁨(=joy)
	▶ It's my _____
5	육지, 땅
6	죄, 죄악, 잘못
10	기쁜, 반가운
	▶ (I'm) _____ to meet you
13	언제
	▶ say _____ 됐으면 말해

정답은 책의 뒤편에서 확인하세요

MEMO

Standing on the Promise

Standing on the promises of Christ my King,
Through eternal ages let His praises ring,
Glory in the highest, I will shout and sing,
Standing on the promises of God

(refrain) Standing, standing,
Standing on the promises of God(or Christ) my Savior;
Standing, standing,
I'm standing on the promises of God

Standing on the promises that cannot fail,
When the howling storms of doubt and fear assail,
By the living Word of God I shall prevail,
Standing on the promises of God

------- refrain -------

Standing on the promises I cannot fall,
Listening every moment to The Spirit's call,
Resting in my Savior As my all in all,
Standing on the promises of God

------- refrain × 2 -------

◇ QR코드를 스캔하여 유튜브로 들어보세요!!

◇ 유튜브(www.youtube.com) 검색창에 아래와 같이 입력하고 돋보기를
클릭해도 됩니다.

Standing on the Promise Alan Jackson | 🔍

노래 알아보기

우리나라에서는 '주의 약속하신 말씀 위에서'로 번역되어 불리고 있으며 찬송가 399장 이기도 한 이곡은 러셀 켈소 카터(Russell Kelso Carter, 1849~1928) 목사님이 로마서 4장 20, 21절을 바탕으로 작사·작곡 하였고 존 스웨니(John R. Sweney)와 카터 목사가 편집한 'Song of Perfect Love(완전한 사랑의 노래)'에 처음 수록되었습니다.

카터 목사는 미국 매릴랜드에서 태어나 펜실베니아주 사관학교를 수석 졸업하고 사관학교에서 토목공학과 공업수학을 가르치는 교수로 재직하던 중 이곡을 작곡하였고 이후에 목사로도 안수를 받았습니다. 카터 목사는 수학, 과학 등 다양한 분야에 대해 연구하였는데 말년에는 의학을 공부하고 의사면허를 취득하였고 기도에 의한 치유경험을 바탕으로 믿음에 의한 질병의 치유에 관한 책을 저술하기도 하였습니다.

행진곡풍의 이곡을 들어보면 평소 활달한 성격으로 알려진 사관학교 교수 출신 카터 목사님의 구원에 대한 굳센 믿음이 느껴지는 것 같습니다.

이곡은 최근까지 여러 가지 버전으로 불리고 있는데 특히 미국 컨트리 가수인 앨런 잭슨(Alan Jackson)이 부른 이 찬송을 들어보면 컨트리 음악 특유의 흥겨움을 느낄 수 있고, CCM 그룹 셀라(Selah)가 부른 곡을 들어보면 재즈 특유의 율동감이 느껴집니다.

노래 배우기

Standing on the promises of Christ my King,

standing 일어선, 일어서고 있는, 고정적인, 변하지 않는
▶ standing room 입석 ▶ standing ovation 기립박수
on ~ 위에
promise 약속 ▶ great and precious promise 크고 귀중한 약속
king 왕, 여기서는 대문자로 시작하므로 하나님으로 해석합니다

Through eternal ages let His praises ring,

through (무엇을, 누구를)통해서, 겪으면서 ▶ I can do everything through Him who gives me strength 나에게 힘을 주시는 그(하나님) 안에서 내가 모든 것을 할 수 있다 (빌립보서 4:13)
eternal 영원한 ▶ **eternity** 영원, 오랜 시간 ▶ **eternal life** 영생
age 나이, 시기
▶ **Iron age** 철기 시대 ▶ **Bronze age** 청동기 시대 ▶ **Stone age** 석기 시대

let ~ 하게 하다
> ▶ let me be the light of the world 내가 세상의 빛이 되게 하소서
praise 칭찬, 찬송, 칭찬하다, 찬송하다
ring (종이)울리다, 전화를 걸다, 반지

Glory in the highest, I will shout and sing,

Glory 영광 ▶ **glorious** 영광스런 ▶ **glorify** 영광스럽게 하다
in ~ 안에 ↔ **out** ~ 밖에
the highest 가장 높은 ↔ **the lowest** 가장 낮은
I will [아이윌]이 아닌 [아일] 이라고 발음해야 노래가 부드럽게 넘어갑니다
shout 소리 지르다, 함성 ▶ shout for(with) joy 기뻐서 소리 지르다
sing 노래하다(sing-sang-sung), 노래

Standing on the promises of God

(refrain) Standing, standing,

refrain 후렴
Standing on the promises of God my Savior;

savior 구세주, 구원자

Standing, standing,

I'm standing on the promises of God

Standing on the promises that cannot fail,

fail 실패하다(↔succeed 성공하다), ~하지 않다 ▶ **failure** 실패(↔success 성공), 불이행

When the howling storms of doubt and fear assail,

howling (바람, 폭풍 등이)울부짖는, 휘몰아치는, 엄청난, 미친듯한
storm 폭풍우 ▶ **stormy** 폭풍우가 몰아치는
> ▶ 속담 After a storm comes a calm. 폭풍우 후에 고요함이 온다(苦盡甘來, 고진감래)
doubt 의심 ▶ **doubtful** 의심스런 ▶ **doubtless** 의심없이, 틀림없이
fear 두려움 ▶ **fearful** 두려운 ▶ **fearless** 두려움 없는
assail 공격하다(=attack), 괴롭히다

By the living Word of God I shall prevail,

by ~에 의해서 ▶ by로 시작하는 부사구를 뒤로 돌리면 I shall prevail by the living word of God입니다

living 살아있는 ▶ **living room**(= family room) 거실

word 단어, 여기서는 대문자로 시작하기 때문에 '하나님의 말씀'이라고 해석합니다

I shall ~ 나는 ~을 하리라 ▶ **I will** ~ 나는 ~을 할 것이다

prevail 우세하다, 만연하다, 승리하다, 이기다

▶ 속담 Truth will prevail 진리는 승리한다

Standing on the promises of God

refrain

Standing on the promises I cannot fall,

fall 넘어지다, 떨어지다, 추락하다, 가을

▶ fallen 넘어진 ▶ fallen angel 추락한(타락한) 천사

Listening every moment to The Spirit's call,

listen 듣다 ▶ listen은 소리를 목적을 가지고 주의 깊게 듣는 경우에 사용됩니다

▶ listen and answer 듣고 답하세요

every 모든 ▶ **every word** 모든 말 ▶ **every part** 모든 부분

moment 순간 ▶ **wait a moment** 잠시만 기다려줘

spirit 성령, 영혼, 정신 ▶ **spiritual** 성령의, 영혼의, 정신의

call 부름 ▶ **calling** 소명, 직업

Resting in my Savior As my all in all

rest 휴식 ▶ **resting** 쉬는, 쉬고 있는 ▶ **restless** 쉼 없는

Savior 구세주

as ~로서 ~처럼 ~할 때 ~하면서

▶ as for me 나로서는 ▶ as time goes by 시간이 흐르면서

all in all 전부(=everything), 전체로, 전면적으로, 완전히, 대체로

Standing on the promises of God

refrain × 2

🎵 노래 배우기(REmind)

아래와 같이 앞서 배웠던 단어나 문구의 뜻을 말해보고 각자 문장을 만들어 보세요!!

Standing on the promises of Christ my King,

standing *일어선* ▶ **standing room** *입석* ▶ **standing ovation** *기립박수*

on ~ *위에*

promise *약속* ▶ great and precious promise *크고 귀중한 약속*

Through eternal ages let His praises ring,

through ＿＿＿＿ ▶ I can do everything ＿＿＿ Him who gives me strength

eternal ＿＿＿ ▶ **eternity** ＿＿＿ ▶ **eternal life** ＿＿＿

age ＿＿＿

▶ **Iron age** ＿＿＿ ▶ **Bronze age** ＿＿＿ ▶ **Stone age** ＿＿＿

let ＿＿＿ ▶ let me be the light of the world ＿＿＿

praise ＿＿＿

ring ＿＿＿

Glory in the highest, I will shout and sing,

Glory ＿＿＿ ▶ **glorious** ＿＿＿ ▶ **glorify** ＿＿＿

in ＿＿＿ ↔ **out** ＿＿＿

the highest ＿＿＿ ↔ **the lowest** ＿＿＿

shout ＿＿＿ ▶ shout for(with) joy ＿＿＿

sing ＿＿＿ (**sing - sang -** ＿＿＿)

Standing on the promises of God

(refrain) Standing, standing,

refrain

Standing on the promises of God my Savior;

savior ＿＿＿

Standing, standing,

I'm standing on the promises of God

Standing on the promises that cannot fail,

fail .... ↔ succeed ....

▶ **failure** .... ↔ **success** ....

When the howling storms of doubt and fear assail,

howling ....

storm .... ▶ **stormy** ....

▶ 속담 After a storm comes a ....

doubt .... ▶ **doubtful** .... ▶ **doubtless** ....

fear .... ▶ **fearful** .... ▶ **fearless** ....

assail .... = **attack** ....

By the living Word of God I shall prevail,

living .... ▶ **living room**(= family room) ....

Word ....

I shall .... ▶ **I will** ....

prevail .... ▶ 속담 Truth will prevail ....

Standing on the promises of God

refrain

Standing on the promises I cannot fall,

fall .... ▶ **fallen** .... ▶ **fallen angel** ....

Listening every moment to The Spirit's call,

listen .... ▶ **listen and answer** ....

every .... ▶ **every word** .... ▶ **every part** ....

moment .... ▶ **wait a moment** ....

spirit .... ▶ **spiritual** ....

call .... ▶ **calling** ....

Resting in my Savior As my all in all

rest .... ▶ **resting** .... ▶ **restless** ....

as .... ▶ as for me .... ▶ as time goes by ....

all in all ....

Standing on the promises of God

refrain × 2

영한번역

Standing on the promises of Christ my King	나의 왕 예수님의 약속 위에 굳게 서서
Through eternal ages let His praises ring	영원토록 하나님에 대한 찬송이 울려 퍼지게 하리라
Glory in the highest I will shout and sing	가장 높은 곳에 영광, 나는 소리치며 노래하리
Standing on the promises of God	하나님의 약속 위에 굳게 서리
(refrain) Standing, standing,	(후렴) 굳게 서리, 굳게 서리
Standing on the promises of God(or Christ) my Savior	나의 구세주 하나님(또는 예수님)의 약속 위에 굳게 서서
Standing, standing,	굳게 서리, 굳게 서리
I'm standing on the promises of God	나는 하나님의 약속 위에 굳건하게 서 있네
Standing on the promises that cannot fail,	실패하지 않는(틀림없는) 약속 위에 굳게 서서
When the howling storms of doubt and fear assail,	의심과 두려움의 휘몰아치는 폭풍이 엄습해 올 때
By the living Word of God I shall prevail,	하나님의 살아있는 말씀으로 나는 승리하리라
Standing on the promises of God	하나님의 약속 위에 굳게 서리
refrain	후렴
Standing on the promises I cannot fall,	내가 넘어질 수 없는 약속 위에 굳게 서서
Listening every moment to The Spirit's call,	모든 순간 성령의 부르심에 귀 기울이며
Resting in my Savior As my all in all,	나의 모든 것 되시는 나의 구세주 안에서 쉬면서
Standing on the promises of God	하나님의 약속 위에 굳게 서리
refrain	후렴
refrain	후렴

번역해보기

Standing on the promises of Christ my King

나의 왕 예수님의 약속 위에 굳게 서서

Through eternal ages let His praises ring

Glory in the highest I will shout and sing

Standing on the promises of God

(refrain) Standing, standing,

Standing on the promises of God(or Christ) my Savior

Standing, standing,

I'm standing on the promises of God

Standing on the promises that cannot fail,

When the howling storms of doubt and fear assail,

By the living Word of God I shall prevail,

Standing on the promises of God

refrain

Standing on the promises I cannot fall,

내가 넘어질 수 없는 약속 위에 굳게 서서

Listening every moment to The Spirit's call,

Resting in my Savior As my all in all,

Standing on the promises of God

refrain

refrain

✚ 노래와 관련된 성경 말씀

앞서 배운 영어찬양과 관련된 성경말씀을 알아봅시다!!

Yet he did not waver through unbelief regarding the promise of God, but was strengthened in his faith and gave glory to God, being fully persuaded that God had power to do what he had promised. (Romans 4:20, 21)

믿음이 없어 하나님의 약속을 의심하지 않고 믿음으로 견고하여져서 하나님께 영광을 돌리며 약속하신 그것을 또한 능히 이루실 줄을 확신하였으니 (로마서 4:20, 21)

His divine power has given us everything we need for life and godliness through our knowledge of him who called us by his own glory and goodness.
Through these he has given us his very great and precious promises, so that through them you may participate in the divine nature and escape the corruption in the world caused by evil desires. (2 Peter 1:3-4)

그의 신기한 능력으로 생명과 경건에 속한 모든 것을 우리에게 주셨으니 이는 자기의 영광과 덕으로써 우리를 부르신 이를 앎으로 말미암음이라
이로써 그 보배롭고 지극히 큰 약속을 우리에게 주사 이 약속으로 말미암아 너희가 정욕 때문에 세상에서 썩어질 것을 피하여 신성한 성품에 참여하는 자가 되게 하려 하셨느니라 (베드로후서 1:3-4)

Let us hold unswervingly to the hope we profess, for he who promised is faithful. (Hebrews 10:23)

또 약속하신 이는 미쁘시니 우리가 믿는 도리의 소망을 움직이지 말며 굳게 잡고 (히브리서 10:23)

From this man's descendants God has brought to Israel the Savior Jesus, as he promised (Acts 13:23)

하나님이 약속하신 대로 이 사람의 후손에서 이스라엘을 위하여 구주를 세우셨으니 곧 예수라 (사도행전 13:23)

May your unfailing love come to me, O LORD, your salvation according to your promise (Psalms 119:41)

여호와여 주의 말씀대로 주의 인자하심과 주의 구원을 내게 임하게 하소서 (시편 119:41)

(Romans 4:20, 21) **waver** 망설이다, 동요하다, 흔들리다, 망설임, 동요, 흔들림
(Hebrews 10:23) **unswervingly** 확고하게 / **unswerving** 확고한, 부동의
(Hebrews 10:23) **profess** 공언하다, 고백하다
(Acts 13:23) **descendant** 자손, 후손 ↔ **ancestor** 선조, 조상
(Psalms 119:41) **according to ~** (= **in accordance with ~**) ~ 에 따라서, 에 응하여

앞서 배운 성경말씀을 소리 내어 읽어보고 해석해 보세요!!

Yet he did not waver through unbelief regarding the promise of God, but was strengthened in his faith and gave glory to God, being fully persuaded that God had power to do what he had promised. (Romans 4:20, 21)

His divine power has given us everything we need for life and godliness through our knowledge of him who called us by his own glory and goodness.
Through these he has given us his very great and precious promises, so that through them you may participate in the divine nature and escape the corruption in the world caused by evil desires. (2 Peter 1:3-4)

Let us hold unswervingly to the hope we profess, for he who promised is faithful. (Hebrews 10:23)

From this man's descendants God has brought to Israel the Savior Jesus, as he promised (Acts 13:23)

May your unfailing love come to me, O LORD, your salvation according to your promise (Psalms 119:41)

Puzzle 6

'STANDING ON THE PROMISE' 에서 배웠던 단어들로 퍼즐을 완성해 봅시다!

Across_가로

- **2** 노래하다
- **4** 약속
- **8** 우세하다, 만연하다, 승리하다, 이기다
  ▶ Truth will _____
- **9** 성령, 영혼, 정신
- **10** 휴식, 휴식하다
- **11** 넘어지다, 떨어지다, 추락하다, 가을
- **12** 폭풍우   ▶ After a _____ comes a calm
- **13** 칭찬, 찬송, 칭찬하다, 찬송하다
- **15** 의심
- **16** 영광   ▶ _____ in the highest
- **17** 왕 ↔ queen

Down_세로

- **1** 나이, 시기   ▶ Ice _____ 빙하시대
- **2** 구세주, 구원자
- **3** 순간, 분
- **5** 모든 것
- **6** 단어
- **7** 빛
- **9** 일어서다
- **14** (종이)울리다, 전화를 걸다, 반지

정답은 책의 뒤편에서 확인하세요

He never sleep*

When you've prayed every prayer that you know how to pray
Just remember the Lord will hear and the answer in on its way
Our God is able
He is mighty
He is faithful

(refrain) And He never sleeps, He never slumbers
He never tires of hearing our prayer
When we are weak, He becomes stronger
So rest in His love and cast all of your cares on Him

Do you feel that the Lord has forgotten your need
Just remember that God is always working in ways you cannot see
Our God is able
He is mighty
He is faithful

------- refrain × 4 -------

◇ QR코드를 스캔하여 유튜브로 들어보세요!!
◇ 유튜브(www.youtube.com) 검색창에 아래와 같이 입력하고 돋보기를 클릭해도 됩니다.

He never sleep don moen   🔍

노래 알아보기

이곡은 앞서 소개되었던 돈 모엔(Don Moen) 목사님이 작사·작곡하신 곡으로 2006년 발표된 앨범인 'Hiding Place(피난처)'에 수록되어 있는 곡입니다. 돈 모엔 목사님은 2006년 일본에서 열린 찬양예배에서 '어느날 나는 내가 매일 밤 하나님께 같은 것을 기도드리고 있음을 깨닫게 되었는데, 하나님은 날마다 같은 기도를 할지라도 우리의 기도를 들어주시는 데 절대로 지치시는 법이 없으셨고 하나님은 절대 잠들지 않는 분이시다'라고 이곡을 소개하셨습니다. 힘들고 지칠 때 언제라도 우리의 기도를 들어주시는 신실하신 하나님을 생각하며 찬양을 불러봅시다.

 노래 배우기

When you've prayed every prayer that you know how to pray

you've = you have
pray 기도하다 ▶ **prayer** 기도 ▶ **the Lord's Prayer** 주기도문
know 알다 ▶ **knowledge** 지식
how to pray 어떻게 기도하는지

Just remember the Lord will hear and the answer in on its way

Just 단지, 다만
remember 기억하다 ▶ **remembrance** 기억(=memory)
lord 주님, 주인
hear 듣다 (hear-heard-heard)
answer 대답하다
way 방법, 방식, 길
on its way ~ 하는 길에, 가는(오는) 중인, 앞으로 일어날 일에

Our God is able

Our God 'r'의 발음이 거의 안 되어 [알가드]라고 들립니다
able 가능한, 능력이 있는 ▶ be able to = can

He is mighty

mighty 힘센 ▶ might 힘

He is faithful

faithful 신실한, 충실한, 성실한 ▶ **faith** 믿음, 신앙

And He never sleeps He never slumbers

never 절대 ~ 아니다
sleep 잠, 수면, 잠자다 ▶ **sleepy** 졸린
slumber 졸다(=doze), 잠자다, (화산 등이 활동을) 멈추다, 잠, 수면
  ▶ slumber party 파자마 파티
  ▶ He never slumber away his life 그는 결코 그의 인생을 졸면서(헛되이) 보내지 않았다

He never tires of hearing our prayer

tire of ~ ~에 지친 ▶ tire of hearing ~ ~을 듣기에 지친

When we are weak He becomes stronger

when ~ ~한때
weak 약한 ▶ **weakness** 약함
stronger 더 힘센 ▶ strong-stronger-strongest 힘센-더 힘센-가장 힘센
  ▶ let the weak say I'm strong 약한 자가 '나는 강하다'라고 말하도록 하라

So rest in His love

and cast all of your cares on Him

so 그러므로
rest 쉬다, 쉼 ▶ **restless** 쉼 없는
  ▶ restless life 쉼 없는 인생(바쁘게 돌아가는 인생)
love 사랑하다, 사랑
cast 던지다, 보내다, (배역을) 맡기다, 던지기, 배역 ▶ **throw** 던지다(대부분 구체적인 물건을 던지는 경우는 throw를, 추상적인 것을 던지는 경우 cast를 사용합니다)
care 걱정(염려), 걱정(염려)하다
  ▶ careless 걱정(근심) 없는 ▶ careful 걱정되는, 주의 깊은

Do you feel that the Lord has forgotten our need

feel 느끼다 ▶ how do you feel? 어떻게 느껴? 뭐라고 생각해?
forget 잊어버리다(forget-forgot-forgotten)

need 필요하다, 필요
> 속담 A friend in need is a friend indeed 필요할 때 친구가 진정한 친구

Just remember that God is always working in ways you cannot see

remember 기억하다 ▶ **remembrance** 기억
always 항상, 언제나
> Rejoice always and pray without ceasing 항상 기뻐하고 쉬지 말고 기도하라
way 방법, 방식, 길

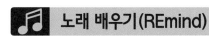 **노래 배우기(REmind)**

아래와 같이 앞서 배웠던 단어나 문구의 뜻을 말해보고 각자 문장을 만들어 보세요!!

When you've prayed every prayer that you know how to pray

pray *기도하다* ▶ **prayer** *기도* ▶ the Lord's Prayer *주기도문*
know *알다* ▶ **knowledge** *지식*
how to pray *어떻게 기도하는지*

Just remember the Lord will hear and the answer in on it's way

Just _____
remember _____ ▶ **remembrance**(= _____)
lord _____
hear _____ (hear- _____ - _____)
answer _____
way _____ ▶ **on it's way** _____

Our God is able

able _____ ▶ **be able to** = _____

He is mighty

mighty .... ▶ might ....

He is faithful

faithful .... ▶ faith ....

And He never sleeps He never slumbers

never ....

sleep .... ▶ sleepy ....

slumber(=doze) .... ▶ slumber party ....

▶ He never slumber away his life ....

He never tires of hearing our prayer

tire of .... ▶ tire of hearing ....

When we are weak He becomes stronger

when ~ ....

weak .... ▶ weakness ....

stronger .... ▶ strong- .... -strongest

▶ let the weak say i'm strong ....

So rest in His love and cast all of your cares on Him

so ....

rest .... ▶ restless .... ▶ restless life ....

love ....

cast .... ▶ throw ....

care .... ▶ careless .... ▶ careful ....

Do you feel that the Lord has forgotten our need

feel .... ▶ how do you feel? ....

forget _____ (**forget** - _____ - _____)
need _____ ▶ 속담 A friend in need is a friend _____

Just remember that God is always working in ways you cannot see

remember _____ ▶ **remembrance** _____

always _____

▶ Rejoice always and pray without ceasing _____

way _____

영한번역

When you've prayed every prayer that you know how to pray

Just remember the Lord will hear and the answer in on it's way

Our God is able

He is mighty

He is faithful

당신이 어떻게 기도하는지 알고 있는 모든 기도를 당신이 기도드릴 때

다만 기억하라, 하나님은 들으실 것이고 앞으로 일어날 일에 대해 응답해주실 것임을

우리의 하나님은 능력이 있으시며

그는 힘이 세시고

그는 신실하시다

(refrain) And He never sleeps, He never slumbers

He never tires of hearing our prayer

When we are weak, He becomes stronger

So rest in His love and cast all of your cares on Him

(후렴) 그리고 그는 절대 잠들지 않으시고, 그는 절대 졸지 않으신다

그는 우리의 기도를 들으시는데 절대 지쳐 하지 않으신다

우리가 약할 때, 그는 더욱 강해지신다

그러므로 그의 사랑 안에서 쉬고, 너의 모든 걱정(염려)을 그에게 맡겨라

Do you feel that the Lord has forgotten your need

Just remember that God is always working in ways you cannot see

Our God is able

He is mighty

He is faithful

당신은 하나님이 당신의 필요를 잊으셨다고 느낍니까

다만 기억하라, 하나님은 당신이 볼 수 없는 방식으로 항상 일하고 계심을

우리의 하나님은 능력이 있으시며

그는 힘이 세시고

그는 신실하시다

refrain X 4

후렴 X 4

* 상기 번역은 영어공부를 위한 해석(직역)이며 공인된 한글 번역곡(가사)은 아님을 알려드립니다

번역해보기

When you've prayed every prayer that you know how to pray
Just remember the Lord will hear and the answer in on it's way
Our God is able
He is mighty
He is faithful

당신이 어떻게 기도하는지 알고 있는 모든 기도를 당신이 기도드릴 때

_____
_____
_____
_____

(refrain) And He never sleeps, He never slumbers
He never tires of hearing our prayer
When we are weak, He becomes stronger
So rest in His love and cast all of your cares on Him

_____
_____
_____
_____

Do you feel that the Lord has forgotten your need
Just remember that God is always working in ways you cannot see
Our God is able
He is mighty
He is faithful

당신은 하나님이 당신의 필요를 잊으셨다고 느낍니까

_____
_____
_____
_____

refrain X 4

_____

✚ 노래와 관련된 성경 말씀

앞서 배운 영어찬양과 관련된 성경말씀을 알아봅시다!!

Do you not know? Have you not heard? The LORD is the everlasting God, the Creator of the ends of the earth. He will not grow tired or weary, and his understanding no one can fathom He gives strength to the weary and increases the power of the weak (Isaiah 40:28~29)

너는 알지 못하였느냐 듣지 못하였느냐 영원하신 하나님 여호와, 땅 끝까지 창조하신 이는 피곤하지 않으시며 곤비하지 않으시며 명철이 한이 없으시며
피곤한 자에게는 능력을 주시며 무능한 자에게는 힘을 더하시나니 (이사야 40:28~29)

May your unfailing love rest upon us, O LORD, even as we put our hope in you (Psalm 33:22)

여호와여 우리가 주께 바라는 대로 주의 인자하심을 우리에게 베푸소서 (시편 33:22)

Cast your cares on the LORD and he will sustain you; he will never let the righteous be shaken (Psalm 55:22)

네 짐을 여호와께 맡기라 그가 너를 붙드시고 의인의 요동함을 영원히 허락하지 아니하시리로다 (시편 55:22)

He will not let your foot slip, he who watches over you will not slumber (Psalm 121:3)

이스라엘을 지키시는 이는 졸지도 아니하시고 주무시지도 아니하시리로다 (시편 121:3)

Ask and it will be given to you; seek and you will find; knock and the door will be opened to you (Matthew 7:7)

구하라 그리하면 너희에게 주실 것이요 찾으라 그리하면 찾아낼 것이요 문을 두드리라 그리하면 너희에게 열릴 것이니 (마태복음 7:7)

Come to me, all you who are weary and burdened, and I will give you rest (Matthew 11:28)

수고하고 무거운 짐 진 자들아 다 내게로 오라 내가 너희를 쉬게 하리라 (마태복음 11:28)

Cast all your anxiety on him because he cares for you (1 Peter 5:7)

너희 염려를 다 주께 맡기라 이는 그가 너희를 돌보심이라 (베드로전서 5:7)

If we confess our sins, he is faithful and just and will forgive us our sins and purify us from all unrighteousness (1 John 1:9)

만일 우리가 우리 죄를 자백하면 그는 미쁘시고 의로우사 우리 죄를 사하시며 우리를 모든 불의에서 깨끗하게 하실 것이요 (요한일서 1:9)

(Isaiah 40:28) **fathom** 깊이를 재다, 측량하다
           everlasting(= permanent, eternal) 불변의 영원한
           ↔ temporary 일시적인, 임시의, 순간의
(Psalm 33:22) **unfailing** 틀림없는, 확실한, 무한한
(Psalm 55:22) **sustain** 지지하다, 떠받치다, 부양하다
(1 John 1:9) **purify** 깨끗이 하다, 정화하다 / **pure** 순수한, 맑은, 깨끗한

영어성경 말씀을 한글로 해석해 보기

앞서 배운 성경말씀을 소리 내어 읽어보고 해석해 보세요!!

Do you not know? Have you not heard? The LORD is the everlasting God, the Creator of the ends of the earth. He will not grow tired or weary, and his understanding no one can fathom He gives strength to the weary and increases the power of the weak
(Isaiah 40:28~29)

May your unfailing love rest upon us, O LORD, even as we put our hope in you
(Psalm 33:22)

Cast your cares on the LORD and he will sustain you; he will never let the righteous be shaken
(Psalm 55:22)

He will not let your foot slip, he who watches over you will not slumber (Psalm 121:3)

Ask and it will be given to you; seek and you will find; knock and the door will be opened to you
(Matthew 7:7)

Come to me, all you who are weary and burdened, and I will give you rest (Matthew 11:28)

Cast all your anxiety on him because he cares for you (1 Peter 5:7)

If we confess our sins, he is faithful and just and will forgive us our sins and purify us from all unrighteousness (1 John 1:9)

Puzzle 7

'HE NEVER SLEEP' 에서 배웠던 단어들로 퍼즐을 완성해 봅시다!

Across_가로

- **3** 믿음, 신앙
- **5** 잠, 수면, 잠자다
- **8** 기억하다 (=memorize)
- **10** 방법, 방식, 길
- **11** 힘센 ↔ weak
- **12** 듣다
  - ▶ Do you _____ me? 내 말 들리니?

Down_세로

- **1** 던지다, 던지기, 배역 ,(배역을) 맡기다
- **2** 걱정(염려), 걱정(염려)하다
- **4** 가능한, 능력이 있는 (= can = be _____ to)
- **6** 사랑하다, 사랑
- **7** 기도 ▶ the Lord's _____ 주기도문
- **9** 힘 ▶ _____ and magic 힘과 마법
- **10** 약한 ↔ strong
- **13** 졸다 (=doze)

정답은 책의 뒤편에서 확인하세요

MEMO

Amazing grace

Amazing grace! How sweet the sound
That saved a wretch like me!
I once was lost, but now am found
Was blind, but now I see

'Twas grace that taught my heart to fear,
And grace, my fears relieved;
How precious did that grace appear
The hour I first believed!

Through many dangers, toils and snares,
We have already come;
'Tis Grace that brought us safe thus far,
And grace will lead us home.

When we' been there ten thousand years
Bright shining as the sun,
We've no less days to sing God's Praise
Than when we first begun

Amazing grace! How sweet the sound
That saved a wretch like me!
I once was lost, but now am found
Was blind, but now I see

◇ QR코드를 스캔하여 유튜브로 들어보세요!!

◇ 유튜브(www.youtube.com) 검색창에 아래와 같이 입력하고 돋보기를
클릭해도 됩니다.

 amazing grace   Q

🎙️ 노래 알아보기

이곡은 18세기의 가장 위대한 설교자 중 하나인 존 뉴톤(John Newton, 1725~1807) 목사님이 자신의 생애를 돌아보며 1779년에 쓴 찬양시를 바탕으로 작곡 되었습니다. 작곡가는 알려져 있지 않고, 음률은 아일랜드 민요, 스코틀랜드 민요, 또는 북미 체로키 인디언의 민요에서 왔다는 여러 가지 설이 있습니다. 새찬송가 305장(통합 찬송가 405장)에 수록되어 있으며, 우리나라에서는 '나 같은 죄인 살리신'이라는 제목으로 번안되어 불리고 있습니다.

이곡의 작사가인 존 뉴톤은 런던에서 태어나 신앙심이 깊은 어머니 슬하에서 성경 말씀 안에 자랐지만 7살 때 어머니가 돌아가셨고 11살 때부터 바다에서 선원 생활을 시작하면서 하나님을 잊고 범죄와 낭비의 삶을 살기 시작했습니다. 이후 영국 해군에 입대해서 군 생활을 하던 중 힘든 생활을 견디다 못해 탈영하였고 아프리카의 흑인들을 데려다가 노예로 파는 노예상인을 하기도 했습니다. 1748년 영국으로 돌아가는 길에 폭풍우에 배가 좌초되어 며칠 동안 배 안의 물을 퍼내면서 죽을 고비를 넘기며 그는 자기의 삶을 돌아보게 되었고 어렸을 때 배웠던 성경말씀과 하나님에 대한 생각을 하면서 믿음이 자라나게 되었습니다. 이후 회심한 끝에 그의 나이 30대 후반부터 신학공부에 매진하여 영국 성공회 목사가 되었고 이곡을 포함하여 280여 편의 찬송가를 작곡하였습니다. 그의 설교는 매우 유명하여 그의 설교를 듣기 위해 모여든 많은 사람들을 수용할만한 회당이 추가로 마련되었다고 합니다.

그는 또한 젊었을 때 노예상인으로 살았던 삶을 회개하면서 그 당시 당연하게 여겨졌던 노예거래에 대한 폐지를 주장하였고 영국에서 노예 거래를 금지하는 법안(Slave Trade Act 1807)이 통과되는 것을 보고 생을 마감하게 됩니다.

영국 버킹험셔(Buckinghamshire)에 있는 그의 무덤에는 다음과 같은 자필 묘비명이 있다 합니다. "한때 반기독교인이며, 방탕아였고, 아프리카에서 노예들의 종이었던 성직자 존 뉴턴은 우리 주님이시며 구세주이신 예수님의 풍성하신 은혜로 보호되고, 회복되며, 용서받았으며, 그가 없애려고 오랫동안 노력해왔던 믿음을 전파하는 일에 임명되었다."

🎵 노래 배우기

Amazing grace! How sweet the sound

amazing (대단히, 매우) 놀라운, 놀랄만한 ▶ **amaze** (대단히, 매우) 놀라게 하다
grace 은혜, 은총, 우아함, 품위, 예의, 식사 전 기도 ▶ **grace of God** 신의 은혜(은총)
how 얼마나, 어떻게 ▶ How old are you? 당신은 몇 살인가요?
sweet 달콤한 ▶ **bitter** 씁쓸한 ▶ **salty** 짠
sound 소리, 음향 ▶ **sound of bell** 종의 소리
sound 건강한, 건전한
▶ 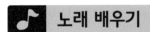 A sound mind in a sound body 건강한 신체에 건전한 마음

That saved a wretch like me!

save (죽음에서, 손실에서) 구하다(= rescue), 안전하게 지키다, 저축하다

wretch 불쌍한 사람, 비열한 사람 ▶ **poor wretch** 가난하고 불쌍한 사람

like ~ ~처럼 ▶ like me 나처럼

I once was lost, but now am found

once 언젠가, 한 번, 이전에, 옛날에

lost (길을, 물건을) 잃어버린 ↔ **found** (find의 과거) 찾은

▶ lost and found 분실물 보관소

now 지금, 현재 ▶ **past** 과거 ▶ **future** 미래

now am found 'I'가 생략되어 있습니다 = now I am found

Was blind, but now I see

was blind = I was blind

blind 눈이 먼, ~을 못 보는, 창문을 가리는 가리개

▶ 속담 Avarice blind our eyes 탐욕은 우리의 눈을 멀게 한다

see 보다(see-saw-seen)

'Twas grace that taught my heart to fear,

'Twas [퉈스]라고 발음됩니다 = It was

that 관계대명사로서 뒤에 나온 문장이 that 앞에 나온 단어(여기서는 grace)를 꾸며줍니다

taught 가르쳤다(teach-taught-taught)

heart 마음, 심장 ▶ heartbeat 심장박동

fear 두려워하다, 두려움

▶ Fear of the Lord is the beginning of the knowledge 하나님을 두려워함이 지식의 시작이다 (잠언 1장 7절)

And grace, my fears relieved;

relieve (고통 등을) 덜어주다, 완화하다

and grace, my fears relieved = and it was grace that relieved my fears

How precious did that grace appear

precious 귀중한, 소중한

appear 나타나다 ▶ appearance 나타남, 외모

▶ 속담 Never judge someone by their appearance 외모로 누군가를 판단하지 말라 (= Beauty is but skin deep)

The hour I first believed!

hour 1시간, 1시간 정도의 시간 ▶ **rush hour** 출퇴근 혼잡 시간대 ▶ **zero hour** 공격 등의 개시 시간
first 최초의, 첫째, 먼저 ▶ **first fruit** 첫 열매

Through many dangers, toils and snares,

through ~ (무엇을, 누구를)통해서, 겪으면서 ▶ I can do everything through Him who gives me
strength 나에게 힘을 주시는 그(하나님) 안에서 내가 모든 것을 할 수 있다 (빌립보서 4:13)
danger 위험 ▶ **dangerous** 위험한
toil 수고, 고역, 힘든 일
snare 덫(=trap), 올무, 올가미, 유혹

I have already come;

already 벌써, 이미
come (어떤 위치나 장소에) 다다르다, 오다

'Tis Grace that brought me safe thus far,

'Tis [티스] = it is
brought 가져왔다(bring-brought-brought)
safe 안전한 ▶ **safety** 안전
thus far 이제까지, 여태까지 (= so far)
It is A that B (강조의 표현으로) B 한 것은 바로 A 이다

And grace will lead me home.

lead 안내하다, 이끌다(lead-led-led), 선두, 앞섬
home 집, 고향, 가정, 본향(천국)
▶ 속담 However humble it may be, there is no place like home
아무리 누추해도 집만 한 곳은 없다

When we' been there ten thousand years

we' been = we have been
there 거기
thousand 천, 1000 ▶ ten thousand years 만년

Bright shining as the sun,

bright 밝은, 환한, 밝게, 환하게 ▶ **bright color** 밝은 색

shining 빛나는, 반짝이는, 밝은 ▶ **a shining future** 빛나는 미래 ▶ **shine** 빛나다
as ~ ~처럼

We've no less days to sing God's Praise

we've = we have
no less 적지 않게
praise 찬양, 칭찬, 찬양하다, 칭찬하다 ▶ **songs of praise** 찬송가
　▶ 속담 Praises can make even a whale dance 칭찬은 고래까지도 춤추게 한다

Than when we first begun

than ~ 보다
begun 시작하다(begin)의 과거분사, begin-began-begun

🎵 **노래 배우기(REmind)**

아래와 같이 앞서 배웠던 단어나 문구의 뜻을 말해보고 각자 문장을 만들어 보세요!!

Amazing grace! How sweet the sound

amazing *대단히 놀라운* ▶ **amaze** *대단히 놀라게 하다*
grace *은혜* ▶ **grace of God** *신의 은혜*
how *얼마나* ▶ How old are you? *당신은 몇 살인가요?*
sweet *달콤한* ▶ **bitter** *씁쓸한* ▶ **salty** *짠*
sound *소리* ▶ **sound of bell** *종의 소리*
　▶ **sound body** *건강한 몸*
　▶ 속담 A sound mind in a sound body *건강한 신체에 건전한 마음*

That saved a wretch like me!

save(= rescue) ＿＿＿＿＿＿＿＿＿
wretch ＿＿＿＿＿＿＿ ▶ **poor wretch** ＿＿＿＿＿＿＿
like ~ ＿＿＿＿＿＿ ▶ **like me** ＿＿＿＿＿＿

I once was lost, but now am found

once _____
lost _____ ↔ **found** _____
▶ lost and found _____
now _____ ▶ **past** _____ ▶ **future** _____
now am found = now _____ am found

Was blind, but now I see

was blind = _____ was blind
blind _____ ▶ 속담 Avarice blind our _____
see _____ (see - _____ - _____)

'Twas grace that taught my heart to fear,

that _____
taught _____ (teach-taught- _____)
heart _____ ▶ heartbeat _____
fear _____
▶ Fear of the Lord is the beginning of the knowledge _____

And grace, my fears relieved;

relieve _____

How precious did that grace appear

precious _____
appear _____ ▶ **appearance** _____
▶ 속담 Never judge someone by their _____

The hour I first believed!

hour _____ ▶ **rush hour** _____ ▶ **zero hour** _____
first _____ ▶ **first fruit** _____

Through many dangers, toils and snares,

through _____ ▶ I can do everything _____ him who gives me strength
danger _____ ▶ **dangerous** _____
toil _____
snare(=trap) _____

I have already come;

already _____
come _____

'Tis Grace that brought me safe thus far,

brought _____ (**bring** - _____ - _____)
safe _____ ▶ **safety** _____
thus far(= so far) _____
It is A that B _____

And grace will lead me home.

lead _____ (lead- _____ - _____)
home _____
▶ 속담 However _____ it may be, there is no place like

When we' been there ten thousand years

there _____
thousand _____ ▶ ten thousand years _____

Bright shining as the sun,

bright _____ ▶ **bright color** _____
shining _____ ▶ **a shining future** _____ ▶ **shine** _____
as _____

We've no less days to sing God's Praise

no less than _____
praise _____ ▶ **songs of praise** _____
▶ 속담 Praises can make even a _____ dance

Than when we first begun

than = (no less) than
begun _____ (begin - _____ - begun)

영한번역

Amazing grace! How sweet the sound	놀라운 은혜! 그 소리가 얼마나 달콤한지
That saved a wretch like me!	그것은 나와 같은 몹쓸 사람(불쌍한 사람)을
	구했네
I once was lost, but now am found	나는 한때 (길을) 잃어 버렸으나, 지금은 찾았네
Was blind, but now I see	나는 눈이 멀었었네, 그러나 지금 나는 보네
'Twas grace that taught my heart to fear,	나의 마음에 두려움을 가르쳐 준 것은
	은혜였습니다
And grace, my fears relieved;	그리고 은혜(였네), 나의 두려움을 덜어준(것은)
How precious did that grace appear	그 은혜가 나타난 것이 얼마나 귀중한지
The hour I first believed!	(얼마나 귀중한지) 내가 처음 믿었던 순간!
Through many dangers, toils and snares,	많은 위험들, 힘든 일들, 함정들을 겪으며
We have already come;	우리는 이미 (본향, 천국에) 도달했네
'Tis Grace that brought us safe thus far,	이제까지 우리를 안전하게 이끌었던 것은
	은혜이네
And grace will lead us home.	그리고 은혜는 우리를 본향(아버지의 집,
	천국)으로 인도하네
When we' been there ten thousand years	우리가 거기에서 만년동안(영원토록) 있었을 때
Bright shining as the sun,	태양처럼 밝게 빛나리
We've no less days to sing God's Praise	우리에게는 하나님의 찬양을 노래할 수 있는
	날들이 적지 않네
Than when we first begun	우리가 처음 시작했을 때 보다

번역해보기

Amazing grace! How sweet the sound   놀라운 은혜! 그 소리가 얼마나 달콤한지

That saved a wretch like me!

I once was lost, but now am found

Was blind, but now I see

'Twas grace that taught my heart to fear,

And grace, my fears relieved;

How precious did that grace appear

The hour I first believed!

Through many dangers, toils and snares,   많은 위험들, 힘든 일들, 함정들을 겪으며

We have already come;

'Tis Grace that brought us safe thus far,

And grace will lead us home.

When we' been there ten thousand years

Bright shining as the sun,

We've no less days to sing God's Praise

Than when we first begun

✝ 노래와 관련된 성경 말씀

앞서 배운 영어찬양과 관련된 성경말씀을 알아봅시다!!

John testifies concerning him. He cries out, saying, "This was he of whom I said, 'He who comes after me has surpassed me because he was before me.' "
From the fullness of his grace we have all received one blessing after another.
For the law was given through Moses; grace and truth came through Jesus Christ.
(John 1:15~17)

요한이 그에 대하여 증언하여 외쳐 이르되 내가 전에 말하기를 내 뒤에 오시는 이가 나보다 앞선 것은 나보다 먼저 계심이라 한 것이 이 사람을 가리킴이라 하니라
우리가 다 그의 충만한 데서 받으니 은혜 위에 은혜러라
율법은 모세로 말미암아 주어진 것이요 은혜와 진리는 예수 그리스도로 말미암아 온 것이라 (요한복음 1:15~17)

But by the grace of God I am what I am, and his grace to me was not without effect. No, I worked harder than all of them--yet not I, but the grace of God that was with me.
(1 Corinthians 15:10)

그러나 내가 나 된 것은 하나님의 은혜로 된 것이니 내게 주신 그의 은혜가 헛되지 아니하여 내가 모든 사도보다 더 많이 수고하였으나 내가 한 것이 아니요 오직 나와 함께 하신 하나님의 은혜로라 (고린도전서 15:10)

who has saved us and called us to a holy life--not because of anything we have done but because of his own purpose and grace. This grace was given us in Christ Jesus before the beginning of time. (2 Timothy 1:9)

하나님이 우리를 구원하사 거룩하신 소명으로 부르심은 우리의 행위대로 하심이 아니요 오직 자기의 뜻과 영원 전부터 그리스도 예수 안에서 우리에게 주신 은혜대로 하심이라 (디모데후서 1:9)

In him we have redemption through his blood, the forgiveness of sins, in accordance with the riches of God's grace. (Ephesians 1:7)

우리는 그리스도 안에서 그의 은혜의 풍성함을 따라 그의 피로 말미암아 속량 곧 죄 사함을 받았느니라 (에베소서 1:7)

But because of his great love for us, God, who is rich in mercy, made us alive with Christ even when we were dead in transgressions--it is by grace you have been saved. (Ephesians 2:4~5)

긍휼이 풍성하신 하나님이 우리를 사랑하신 그 큰 사랑을 인하여 허물로 죽은 우리를 그리스도와 함께 살리셨고 (너희는 은혜로 구원을 받은 것이라) (에베소서 2:4~5)

For it is by grace you have been saved, through faith--and this not from yourselves, it is the gift of God. (Ephesians 2:8)

너희는 그 은혜에 의하여 믿음으로 말미암아 구원을 받았으니 이것은 너희에게서 난 것이 아니요 하나님의 선물이라 (에베소서 2:8)

And everyone who calls on the name of the Lord will be saved.' (Acts 2:21)

누구든지 주의 이름을 부르는 자는 구원을 받으리라 하였느니라 (사도행전 2:21)

(John 1:15) **surpass** ~ 를 넘어서다(능가하다)
(Ephesians 1:7) **in accordance with** ~ (= according to ~) ~ 에 따라, ~ 에 일치하여
(Ephesians 2:5) **transgression** 허물, 범죄
(Acts 2:21) **call on** ~ 를 부르다, ~ 를 방문하다

앞서 배운 성경말씀을 소리 내어 읽어보고 해석해 보세요!!

John testifies concerning him. He cries out, saying, "This was he of whom I said, 'He who comes after me has surpassed me because he was before me.' "
From the fullness of his grace we have all received one blessing after another.
For the law was given through Moses; grace and truth came through Jesus Christ. (John 1:15~17)

But by the grace of God I am what I am, and his grace to me was not without effect. No, I worked harder than all of them--yet not I, but the grace of God that was with me. (1 Corinthians 15:10)

who has saved us and called us to a holy life--not because of anything we have done but because of his own purpose and grace. This grace was given us in Christ Jesus before the beginning of time. (2 Timothy 1:9)

In him we have redemption through his blood, the forgiveness of sins, in accordance with the riches of God's grace. (Ephesians 1:7)

But because of his great love for us, God, who is rich in mercy, made us alive with Christ even when we were dead in transgressions--it is by grace you have been saved. (Ephesians 2:4~5)

For it is by grace you have been saved, through faith--and this not from yourselves, it is the gift of God. (Ephesians 2:8)

And everyone who calls on the name of the Lord will be saved. (Acts 2:21)

Puzzle 8

☀ 'AMAZING GRACE' 에서 배웠던 단어들로 퍼즐을 완성해 봅시다!

Across_가로

1. 안전한
3. 그러나 ↔ and
5. 가르치다 ↔ learn
7. 귀중한, 소중한 ▶ my _____
9. 열, 10
12. (대단히, 매우) 놀라운, 놀랄만한
14. 위험
15. 구조하다 (=save)
17. 집, 고향, 가정, 본향
   ▶ However humble it may be, there is no place like _____
18. 소리, 음향, 건강한, 건전한

Down_세로

2. 나타남, 외모
   ▶ Never judge someone by their _____
4. 천, 1000
6. 시작하다
8. 덫 (=trap), 올무, 올가미, 유혹
9. 수고, 고역, 힘든 일
10. 달콤한 ▶ _____ potato (고구마)
11. 밝은, 환한, 밝게, 환하게
13. 은혜, 은총, 우아함, 품위, 예의, 식전 기도
16. (길을, 물건을) 잃어버린
   ▶ _____ and found (분실물 보관소)
17. 시간 ▶ rush _____ 출퇴근 혼잡한 시간

정답은 책의 뒤편에서 확인하세요

There is none like You*

There is none like You
No one else can touch my heart like You do
I could search for all eternity, Lord
And find there is none like You

(refrain) There is none like You
No one else can touch my heart like You do
I could search for all eternity, Lord
And find there is none like You

Your mercy flows like a river wide,
And healing comes from Your hand
Suffering children are safe in Your arms
There is none like You

-------refrain ×2 -------

I could search for all eternity Lord
And find there is none like You

There is none, ×2

There is none like You

◇ QR코드를 스캔하여 유튜브로 들어보세요!!

◇ 유튜브(www.youtube.com) 검색창에 아래와 같이 입력하고 돋보기를
클릭해도 됩니다.

There is none like You lenny leblanc | 🔍

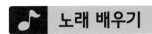 **노래 알아보기**

'주님과 같이'로 번안되어 우리나라에서도 널리 불리고 있는 이곡은 미국의 찬양사역자 레니 르블랑 (Lenny LeBlanc, 1951~)이 작사·작곡 하였습니다. 르블랑은 그의 친구인 피트 카(Pete Carr)와 같이 르블랑 앤 카(LeBlanc & Carr)라는 그룹으로 'Falling'이라는 곡을 히트시키며 70년대 후반 엄청난 인기를 누렸습니다. 그런데 1980년 어느 날 밤 한때 마약밀매업자였던 그의 친한 친구가 찾아와 그에게 "레니 나는 구원을 받았고 천국에 갈 거야. 나는 너도 나와 함께 천국에 가길 원해. 너는 구원받았니?"라고 물었고 레니는 생각할 틈도 없이 "yes"라고 답했다고 합니다. 그 친구는 레니에게 성경책을 보냈고 레니는 그로부터 몇 주 동안 하나님께서 지극하신 사랑을 자신에게 보여주심을 느끼며 자신의 이기적이고 깊이 없던 삶에 대해 깨닫게 되고 하나님 앞에서 울며 자비와 용서를 구했다 합니다. 그로부터 레니는 그동안의 팝음악에서의 성공적인 경력을 내려놓고 예수님 안에서 발견한 믿음에 관한 곡을 작곡하며 찬양 리더로 활동하기 시작했으며 이곡과 Above All(우리나라 번안곡 이름으로는 '모든 능력과 모든 권세') 등 유명한 곡을 다수 남기며 꾸준한 활동을 하고 있습니다.

♪ 노래 배우기

There is none like You

there 저기 ▶ there is ~ ~이 있다
none 아무도(~않다), 전혀~아니다
like ~처럼, ~와 같이, 좋아하다 ▶ He is like a tree 그는 나무와 같다

No one else can touch my heart like You do

else 또 다른 ▶ anything else 그밖에 무언가 ▶ something else 무언가 다른 중요한 것
can 가능하다(=be able to)
touch 만지다, 건드리다
heart 심장, 마음
like you 당신처럼 ▶ like you do 당신이 하는 것처럼

I could search for all eternity, Lord

search for ~ ~를 찾다 ▶ seek 찾기, 찾다, 추구하다 ▶ hide and seek 숨바꼭질
eternity 영원, 오랜 시간 ▶ eternal 영원한 ▶ eternal life 영생
lord 주님, 군주

And find, there is none like You

find (우연히) 찾다 ▶ find out 발견하다, 알아내다, 간파하다
none (=no one) 아무도

(refrain) There is none like You
refrain 후렴

No one else can touch my heart like You do
I could search for all eternity Lord
And find, there is none like You
Your mercy flows like a river wide

mercy 자비 ▶ merciful 자비로운 ▶ works of mercy 자선행위
▶ it's a mercy 다행이다
flow (물 등의)흐름, 흐르다, 몰입
river 강, 하천 ▶ stream 시내, 개울
wide 넓은 ▶ width 폭 ▶ river wide = wide river 넓은 강

And healing comes from Your hand

healing 치유 ▶ heal 치료하다(=cure)
come from ~ ~로부터 오다

Suffering children are safe in Your arms

suffering 고통(고난)받고 있는, 고통, 고난 ▶ suffer 고통받다, 시달리다, (안좋은 것을)겪다
children 아이들 ▶ child 아이
safe 안전한 ▶ safety 안전
arm 팔, 무기, 무장
▶ God who arms me with strength 힘으로 나를 무장시키시는 하나님

refrain ×2
I could search for all eternity, Lord
And find there is none like You
There is none, ×2
There is none like You

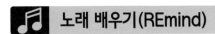 노래 배우기(REmind)

아래와 같이 앞서 배웠던 단어나 문구의 뜻을 말해보고 각자 문장을 만들어 보세요!!

There is none like You

there *저기* ▶ **there is ~** *~이 있다*
none *아무도*
like *~처럼* ▶ **He is like a tree** *그는 나무와 같다*

No one else can touch my heart like You do

else ▶ anything else ▶ something else
can(=be able to)
touch
heart
like you ▶ like you do

I could search for all eternity, Lord

search for ▶ seek ▶ hide and seek
eternity ▶ eternal ▶ eternal life
lord

And find, there is none like You

find ▶ find out
none(=no one)

(refrain) There is none like You

refrain

No one else can touch my heart like You do

I could search for all eternity Lord

And find, there is none like You

Your mercy flows like a river wide

mercy ▶ merciful
  ▶ works of mercy   ▶ it's a mercy
flow
river   ▶ stream
wide   ▶ width

And healing comes from Your hand

healing   ▶ heal(=cure)
come from

Suffering children are safe in Your arms

suffering   ▶ suffer
children   ▶ child
safe   ▶ safety
arm   ▶ God who arms me with strength

refrain

refrain

I could search for all eternity, Lord

And find there is none like You

There is none, There is none,

There is none like You

영한번역

There is none like You	당신과 같은 분은 없습니다
No one else can touch my heart like You do	아무도 당신(이 그러는 것)처럼 내 마음을 만지는 분은 없습니다
I could search for all eternity, Lord	나는 오랫동안 모든 영원한 것을 찾아보았습니다, 주님
And find there is none like You.	그리고 알았습니다 당신과 같은 분은 없다는 것을

(refrain) There is none like You	(후렴) 당신과 같은 분은 없습니다
No one else can touch my heart like You do	아무도 당신(이 그러는 것)처럼 내 마음을 만지는 분은 없습니다
I could search for all eternity, Lord	나는 오랫동안 모든 영원한 것을 찾아보았습니다, 주님
And find there is none like You	그리고 알았습니다 당신과 같은 분은 없다는 것을

Your mercy flows like a river wide,	당신의 자비가 넓은 강물과 같이 흐릅니다
And healing comes from Your hand	그리고 치유가 당신의 손으로부터 옵니다
Suffering children are safe in Your arms	고통받는 아이들은 당신의 팔안에서 안전합니다
There is none like You	당신과 같은 분은 없습니다

refrain × 2	후렴 × 2

I could search for all eternity, Lord	나는 오랫동안 모든 영원한 것을 찾았습니다, 주님
And find there is none like You	그리고 찾았습니다 당신과 같은 분은 없다는 것을
There is none,	아무도,
There is none,	아무도,
There is none like You.	당신과 같은 분은 없습니다

※ 상기 번역은 영어공부를 위한 해석(직역)이며 공인된 한글 번역곡(가사)은 아님을 알려드립니다

번역해보기

There is none like You

No one else can touch my heart like You do

I could search for all eternity, Lord

And find there is none like You.

당신과 같은 분은 없습니다

(refrain) There is none like You

No one else can touch my heart like You do

I could search for all eternity, Lord

And find there is none like You

Your mercy flows like a river wide,

And healing comes from Your hand

Suffering children are safe in Your arms

There is none like You

당신의 자비가 넓은 강물과 같이 흐릅니다

refrain × 2

I could search for all eternity, Lord

And find there is none like You

There is none,

There is none,

There is none like You.

노래와 관련된 성경 말씀

앞서 배운 영어찬양과 관련된 성경말씀을 알아봅시다!!

Hear my prayer, O LORD; listen to my cry for mercy.
In the day of my trouble I will call to you, for you will answer me.
Among the gods there is none like you, O Lord; no deeds can compare with yours.
(Psalm 86:6~8)

여호와여 나의 기도에 귀를 기울이시고 내가 간구하는 소리를 들으소서
나의 환난 날에 내가 주께 부르짖으리니 주께서 내게 응답하시리이다
주여 신들 중에 주와 같은 자 없사오며 주의 행하심과 같은 일도 없나이다. (시편 86:6~8)

"How great you are, Sovereign LORD! There is no one like you, and there is no God but you, as we have heard with our own ears. (2 Samuel 7:22)

그런즉 주 여호와여 이러므로 주는 위대하시니 이는 우리 귀로 들은 대로는 주와 같은 이가 없고 주 외에는 신이 없음이니이다. (사무엘하 7:22)

No one is like you, LORD; you are great, and your name is mighty in power. (Jeremiah 10:6)

여호와여 주와 같은 이 없나이다 주는 크시니 주의 이름이 그 권능으로 말미암아 크시니이다. (예레미아 10:6)

His mercy extends to those who fear him, from generation to generation. (Luke 1:50)

긍휼하심이 두려워하는 자에게 대대로 이르는도다 (누가복음 1:50)

Praise be to the God and Father of our Lord Jesus Christ! In his great mercy he has given us new birth into a living hope through the resurrection of Jesus Christ from the dead (1 Peter 1:3)

우리 주 예수 그리스도의 아버지 하나님을 찬송하리로다 그의 많으신 긍휼대로 예수 그리스도를 죽은 자 가운데서 부활하게 하심으로 말미암아 우리를 거듭나게 하사 산 소망이 있게 하시며 (베드로전서 1:3)

🔊 영어성경 말씀을 한글로 해석해 보기

앞서 배운 성경말씀을 소리 내어 읽어보고 해석해 보세요!!

Hear my prayer, O LORD; listen to my cry for mercy.
In the day of my trouble I will call to you, for you will answer me.
Among the gods there is none like you, O Lord; no deeds can compare with yours.
(Psalm 86:6~8)

_____

_____

_____

"How great you are, Sovereign LORD! There is no one like you, and there is no God but you, as we have heard with our own ears. (2 Samuel 7:22)

_____

_____

_____

No one is like you, LORD; you are great, and your name is mighty in power. (Jeremiah 10:6)

_____

_____

His mercy extends to those who fear him, from generation to generation. (Luke 1:50)

_____

_____

Praise be to the God and Father of our Lord Jesus Christ! In his great mercy he has given us new birth into a living hope through the resurrection of Jesus Christ from the dead (1 Peter 1:3)

_____

_____

_____

Puzzle 9

'THERE IS NONE LIKE YOU' 에서 배웠던 단어들로 퍼즐을 완성해 봅시다!

<table>
<tr><td colspan="2">Across_가로</td><td colspan="2">Down_세로</td></tr>
</table>

Across_가로

- **3** 치료하다 (=cure)
- **6** 자비 ▶ it's a _____ 다행이다
- **7** 강, 하천
- **8** 영원한 ▶ _____ life 영생
- **12** 넓은 ↔ narrow
- **14** 주님, 군주

Down_세로

- **1** 아이들
- **2** 만지다, 건드리다
- **4** 팔, 무기, 무장
- **5** 시내, 개울, 흐름
- **9** (=no one) 아무도, 노래 제목에서 찾아보세요
- **10** ~ 처럼, ~ 와 같이, 좋아하다
- **11** 찾다, 발견하다
- **13** (물 등의)흐름, 흐르다, 몰입

You will never walk alone*

Along life's road
There will be sunshine and rain
Roses and thorns, laughter and pain
And 'cross the miles
You will face mountains so steep
Deserts so long and valleys so deep

Sometimes the Journey's gentle
Sometimes the cold winds blow
But I want you to remember
I want you to know

(refrain) You will never walk alone
As long as you have faith
Jesus will be right beside you all the way
And you may feel you're far from home
But home is where He is
And He'll be there down every road
You will never walk alone

never, no never

The path will wind
And you will find wonders and fears
Labors of love and a few falling tears

Across the years
There will be some twists and turns
Mistakes to make and lessons to learn

Sometimes the journey's gentle
Sometimes the cold winds blow
But I want you to remember wherever you may go

------- refrain -------

Jesus knows your joy,
Jesus knows your need
He will go the distance with you faithfully

You will never walk alone
He will be right beside you all the way
When you feel you're far from home
He'll be there down every road

------- refrain -------

never, no never
You never oh you never
never walk alone
you~

◇ QR코드를 스캔하여 유튜브로 들어보세요!!
◇ 유튜브(www.youtube.com) 검색창에 아래와 같이 입력하고 돋보기를
클릭해도 됩니다.

You will never walk alone point of grace 🔍

🎙️ 노래 알아보기

이곡은 로웰 알렉산더(Lowell Alexander)가 작곡하였고 여성 CCM 그룹인 Point of Grace가 불렀습니다. Point of grace는 아칸소(arkansas)주 아카델피아(Arkadelphia)의 우아치타 뱁티스트 대학(Ouachita Baptist University)에서 여성보컬그룹으로 활동하던 12명 중 3명이 1991년에 아카펠라 그룹을 결성하면서 시작되었습니다

1993년에 그룹 이름과 같은 이름의 앨범인 'Point of grace'를 발표하며 정식으로 데뷔하였고 처음 멤버는 쉘리 브린(Shelley Breen), 데니스 존스(Denise Jones), 테리 존스(Terry Jones), 헤더 페인(Heather Payne)이었습니다. 이후 테리는 2003년에 셋째 아이 출산을 위해 은퇴하였고 테리를 대신하여 2004년에 새로운 멤버로 리 캐플리노(Leigh Cappillino)가 영입되었으며 2008년에는 헤더가 그녀의 네 아이와 시간을 더욱 보내고 가정을 돌보기 위해 은퇴하여 현재까지 쉘리, 데니스, 리 3인조 여성 트리오(trio)로 활동하고 있습니다.

Point of grace는 93년 데뷔 이후 도브상(Dove award)을 5번이나 수상하였으며 이곡은 2001년 5월에 발표한 다섯 번째 정식 앨범인 'free to fly'에 수록된 곡입니다.

Point of Grace는 2002년부터 소녀들의 삶에 변화를 주고자 하는 소명으로 10대 소녀들을 삶을 바르게 이끌기 위한 세미나, 저술, 콘서트 등으로 이루어진 'Girls of Grace'라는 이름의 기독교 사역을 하고 있으며 기독교 아동 지원 단체인 컴패션(compassion international)에서 후원활동도 하고 있습니다.

🎵 노래 배우기

Along life's road

> **along** ~을 따라서
> **life** 인생, 삶, 생명 ▶ **eternal life** 영원한 생명
> **road** 길 > path 비교적 좁은 길

There will be sunshine and rain

> **there** 거기 ↔ **here** 여기
> **There will be** ~ : 거기에 ~이 있을 것이다
> **sunshine** 햇살, 햇빛 ▶ sunny 화창한
> ▶ 속담 Make hay while the sun shines 해가 화창할 때 풀을 말려라
> **rain** 비 ▶ rainy 비가 오는

Roses and thorns, laughter and pain

Roses and thorns, laughter and pain = (There will be) roses and thorns, (There will be) laughter and pain

rose 장미

thorn 가시 ▶ crown of thorns 가시관

▶ 속담 No rose without thorn 가시 없는 장미는 없다

laughter 웃음 ▶ **laugh** 웃다

pain 아픔 ▶ **painful** 아픈

▶ 속담 No pains, no gains 수고 없이 얻는 것이 없다

And 'cross the miles

'cross = across 건너서, 가로질러

mile 길이의 단위 ▶ 1 mile 은 약 1.6 km ▶ miles 긴 거리

across the miles : 긴 거리를 건너가다 보면

You will face mountains so steep

face 마주치다, 얼굴 ▶ face to face 얼굴과 얼굴을 마주하여

mountain 산

so 매우

steep 가파른, 경사진 ▶ slope, inclination 경사

Deserts so long and valleys so deep

desert 사막

long 긴 ↔ short 짧은　　속담 Art is long, life is short 예술은 길고, 인생은 짧다

valley 계곡

deep 깊은 ▶ **depth** 깊이

Sometimes the Journey's gentle

sometimes 어떤 때는

journey 여행

gentle 온화한(=mild) ▶ **gentleman** 신사

Sometimes the cold winds blow

cold 차가운 ↔ **hot** 뜨거운

wind 바람 ▶ **windy** 바람이 부는

blow (바람이, 입으로) 불다, (권투 등에서) 타격

But I want you to remember

want 목적어 to 부정사 : 목적어가 ~ 하기를 원하다
remember 기억하다 ▶ remembrance 기억

I want you to know
(refrain) You will never walk alone

refrain 후렴, 생략
never 절대로
walk 걷다, 걷기, 산책 < **run** 뛰다, 뛰기, 달리기
alone 혼자
▶ 속담 Better be alone than in bad company 나쁜 친구를 사귀는 것보다는 혼자 있는 것이 낫다

As long as you have faith

as long as ~ 하는 한
▶ 속담 As long as there's life, there's hope. 생명이 있는 한 희망이 있다
faith 믿음, 신앙 ▶ faithful 신실한, 충실한, 성실한

Jesus will be right beside you all the way

right 바로, 오른편 ▶ right now 바로 지금
beside~ ~옆에 ▶ Sit beside me, my son 내 옆에 앉아라, 내 아들아
right beside you 바로 너의 옆에
all the way 항상(= always)

And you may feel you're far from home

may 아마도
feel 느끼다 ▶ feeling 느낌
far 먼, 멀리 ▶ far from~ ~로부터 먼
home 집, 집으로 ▶ homeless 노숙자(=집 없는 사람)

But home is where He is

where ~ 어디에

And He'll be there down every road

He'll = He will
down 아래에, 아래로 ↔ up 위에, 위로
every 예외 없이 모든 ▶ **all** 모든 ▶ **whole** 빈틈없이 모두, 완전히

You will never walk alone

never, no never

never 절대로

The path will wind

path 좁은길 < **road** 넓은길
wind [와인드] 길이나 강 등이 굽이치다(wind-wound-wound)
▶ wind [윈드] 바람, 가스, 호흡

And you will find wonders and fears

wonder 놀라움, 놀라운 것, 경이로움, 경이로운 것 ▶ **seven wonders** 세계 7대 불가사의
fear 두려움, 두려워하다 ▶ **fearful** 두려운 ▶ **worry** 걱정하다

Labors of love and a few falling tears

labor 수고, 노력, 노동, 근로
few 소량의, 적은 ▶ **a few** 약간의, 몇 가지의
falling 떨어지는, 추락하는
tear 눈물, 울음, 잡아 뜯다

Across the years

across 건너서, 가로질러
years 수년 동안

There will be some twists and turns

twist 꼬임, (몸, 실 등을) 꼬다
turn 돌다, 우회, 차례, 순서 ▶ **turn left** 왼쪽으로 도세요 ▶ **it's my turn** 내 차례야
twists and turns 우여곡절, 도로의 구불거림

Mistakes to make and lessons to learn

mistake 실수, 잘못 ▶ **by mistake** 실수로
lesson 교훈, 가르침, 수업, 강습
learn 배우다 ▶ learning 배움
▶ 속담 The more you learn, the more you earn 더 많이 배울수록 더 많이 번다
▶ 속담 It is never too late to learn 배우기에는 절대로 늦지 않다

Sometimes the journey's gentle

Sometimes the cold winds blow

But I want you to remember wherever you may go

refrain

Jesus knows your joy,

> **joy** 기쁨 ▶ **joyful** 기쁨이 넘치는

Jesus knows your need

> **need** 필요 ▶ A friend in need is a friend indeed 필요할 때 친구가 진정한 친구

He will go the distance with you faithfully

> **distance** (공간 또는 시간상 떨어져 있는) 거리 ▶ **distant** 멀리 떨어져 있는
> **faithfully** 신실하게, 충실하게, 성실하게 ▶ **faith** 믿음, 신앙

You will never walk alone

He will be right beside you all the way

When you feel you're far from home

He'll be there down every road

refrain

never, no never

You never oh you never

never walk alone

you ~

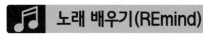

🎵 노래 배우기(REmind)

아래와 같이 앞서 배웠던 단어나 문구의 뜻을 말해보고 각자 문장을 만들어 보세요!!

along life's road

along *~을 따라서*

life *인생, 생명* ▶ **eternal life** *영원한 생명*

road *길* > **path** *비교적 좁은 길*

There will be sunshine and rain

there _____ ↔ **here** _____

There will be _____

sunshine _____ ▶ **sunny** _____

　▶ 속담 Make hay while the sun _____

rain _____ ▶ **rainy** _____

Roses and thorns, laughter and pain

rose _____

thorn _____ ▶ **crown of thorns** _____

　▶ 속담 No rose without thorn _____

laughter _____ ▶ **laugh** _____

pain _____ ▶ **painful** _____

　▶ 속담 No pains, no _____

And 'cross the miles

'cross = across _____

mile _____

You will face mountains so steep

face _____ ▶ **face to face** _____

mountain _____

so _____

steep _____ ▶ **slope**(=inclination) _____

Deserts so long and valleys so deep

desert _____

long _____ ↔ short _____
속담 Art is long, life is short _____
valley _____
deep _____ ▶ depth _____

Sometimes the Journey's gentle

sometimes _____
journey _____
gentle(=mild) _____ ▶ gentleman _____

Sometimes the cold winds blow

cold _____ ↔ hot _____
wind _____ ▶ windy _____
blow _____

But I want you to remember

remember _____ ▶ remembrance _____

I want you to know
(refrain) You will never walk alone

refrain
never _____
walk _____ < run _____
alone
▶ 속담 Better be _____ than in bad company

As long as you have faith

as long as _____
▶ 속담 As long as there's life, there's _____
faith _____ ▶ faithful _____

Jesus will be right beside you all the way

right _____ ▶ right now _____
beside _____ ▶ Sit beside me, my son _____
right beside you _____
all the way(= always) _____

And you may feel you're far from home

may ....
feel .... ▶ feeling
far .... ▶ far from
home .... ▶ homeless

But home is where He is

where ....

And He'll be there down every road

down .... ↔ up ....
every .... ▶ all .... ▶ whole ....

You will never walk alone
never, no never

never ....

The path will wind

path .... < road ....
wind[와인드] .... (wind - .... - ....)
▶ wind[윈드] ....

And you will find wonders and fears

wonder .... ▶ seven wonders ....
fear .... ▶ fearful .... ▶ worry ....

Labors of love and a few falling tears

labor ....
few .... ▶ a few ....
falling ....
tear ....

Across the years

across ....
years ....

There will be some twists and turns

twist _____

turn _____ ▶ **turn left** _____ ▶ **it's my turn** _____

twists and turns _____

Mistakes to make and lessons to learn

mistake _____ ▶ **by mistake** _____

lesson _____

learn _____ ▶ **learning** _____

▶ 속담 The more you learn, the more you _____

▶ 속담 It is never too late to _____

Sometimes the journey's gentle
Sometimes the cold winds blow
But I want you to remember wherever you may go / refrain
Jesus knows your joy,

joy _____ ▶ **joyful** _____

Jesus knows your need

need _____ ▶ A friend in _____ is a friend indeed

He will go the distance with you faithfully

distance _____ ▶ **distant** _____

faithfully _____ ▶ **faith** _____

You will never walk alone
He will be right beside you all the way
When you feel you're far from home
He'll be there down every road / refrain
never, no never
You never oh you never
never walk alone
you ~

영한번역

Along life's road	인생의 길을 따라서 가다 보면
There will be sunshine and rain	햇살도 비도 있을 거예요
Roses and thorns, laughter and pain	장미와 가시, 웃음과 아픔도 있을 거예요
And 'cross the miles	그리고 길을 가다 보면
You will face mountains so steep	당신은 아주 가파른 산을 마주치게 될 것입니다 아주
Deserts so long and valleys so deep	긴 사막과 아주 깊은 계곡(을 당신은 마주치게 될 것입니다)
Sometimes the Journey's gentle	어떤 때는 여행이 온화하고
Sometimes the cold winds blow	어떤 때는 차가운 바람이 붑니다
But I want you to remember	그러나 나는 당신이 기억하길 바랍니다
I want you to know	당신이 알기를 바랍니다
(refrain) You will never walk alone	(후렴) 당신은 절대 혼자 걷지 않을 것입니다
As long as you have faith	당신에게 믿음이 있는 한
Jesus will be right beside you all the way	예수님은 항상 당신의 바로 옆에 있을 것입니다
And you may feel you're far from home	그리고 당신은 아마도 당신이 집으로부터 멀리 떨어져 있다 느낄 것입니다
But home is where He is	그러나 집은 그가 계신 곳입니다
And He'll be there down every road	그리고 그는 모든 길에 계실 것입니다
You will never walk alone	당신은 절대 혼자 걷지 않을 것입니다
never, no never	절대로, 아니 절대로
The path will wind	그 좁은 길은 굽이칠 것입니다
And you will find wonders and fears	그리고 당신은 경이로움과 두려움을 발견할 것입니다
Labors of love and a few falling tears	사랑의 수고와 약간의 떨어지는(흐르는) 눈물들
Across the years	수년을 가로질러서(수년 동안)
There will be some twists and turns	약간의 우여곡절이 있을 것입니다
Mistakes to make and lessons to learn	만들게 되는 실수들과 배워야 할 교훈(이 있을 것입니다)

* 상기 번역은 영어공부를 위한 해석(직역)이며 공인된 한글 번역곡(가사)은 아님을 알려드립니다

Sometimes the journey's gentle | 어떤 때는 여행이 온화하고
Sometimes the cold winds blow | 어떤 때는 차가운 바람이 붑니다
But I want you to remember wherever you may go | 그러나 나는 당신이 기억하길 바랍니다
당신이 어디로 가든지

refrain | 후렴

Jesus knows your joy, | 예수님은 당신의 기쁨을 압니다
Jesus knows your need | 예수님은 당신의 필요를 압니다
He will go the distance with you faithfully | 그는 신실하게 그 먼 길을 당신과 함께 갈 것입니다

You will never walk alone | 당신은 절대 혼자 걷지 않을 것입니다
He will be right beside you all the way | 그가 항상 당신의 바로 옆에 있을 것입니다
When you feel you're far from home | 당신이 집으로부터 멀리 떨어져 있다 느낄 때
He'll be there down every road | 그는 모든 길에 계실 것입니다

refrain | 후렴

never, no never | 절대로, 아니 절대로
You never oh you never | 당신은 절대로 오 당신은 절대로
never walk alone | 절대로 혼자 걷지 않을 것입니다
you ~ | 당신은 ~

Along life's road | 인생의 길을 따라서 가다보면
There will be sunshine and rain
Roses and thorns, laughter and pain
And 'cross the miles
You will face mountains so steep
Deserts so long and valleys so deep

Sometimes the Journey's gentle
Sometimes the cold winds blow
But I want you to remember
I want you to know

(refrain) You will never walk alone
As long as you have faith
Jesus will be right beside you all the way
And you may feel you're far from home
But home is where He is
And He'll be there down every road
You will never walk alone

never, no never

The path will wind | 그 좁은 길은 굽이칠 것입니다
And you will find wonders and fears
Labors of love and a few falling tears
Across the years
There will be some twists and turns
Mistakes to make and lessons to learn

Sometimes the journey's gentle
Sometimes the cold winds blow
But I want you to remember wherever you may
go

refrain

Jesus knows your joy,   예수님은 당신의 기쁨을 압니다
Jesus knows your need
He will go the distance with you faithfully

You will never walk alone
He will be right beside you all the way
When you feel you're far from home
He'll be there down every road

refrain

never, no never
You never oh you never
never walk alone
you ~

✝ 노래와 관련된 성경 말씀

앞서 배운 영어찬양과 관련된 성경말씀을 알아봅시다!!

When Enoch had lived 65 years, he became the father of Methuselah. And after he became the father of Methuselah, <u>Enoch walked with God 300 years</u> and had other sons and daughters. (Genesis 5:21~22)

에녹은 육십오 세에 므두셀라를 낳았고 므두셀라를 낳은 후 <u>삼백 년을 하나님과 동행하며</u> 자녀들을 낳았으며 (창세기 5:21~22)

This is the account of Noah. Noah was a righteous man, blameless among the people of his time, and <u>he walked with God.</u> (Genesis 6:9)

이것이 노아의 족보니라 노아는 의인이요 당대에 완전한 자라 <u>그는 하나님과 동행하였으며</u> (창세기 6:9)

The LORD himself goes before you and will be with you; he will never leave you nor forsake you. Do not be afraid; do not be discouraged. (Deuteronomy 31:8)

그리하면 여호와 그가 네 앞에서 가시며 너와 함께 하사 너를 떠나지 아니하시며 버리지 아니하시리니 너는 두려워하지 말라 놀라지 말라 (신명기 31:8)

Even though I walk through the valley of the shadow of death, I will fear no evil, for you are with me; your rod and your staff, they comfort me. (Psalm 23:4)

내가 사망의 음침한 골짜기로 다닐지라도 해를 두려워하지 않을것은 주께서 나와 함께 하심이라 주의 지팡이와 막대기가 나를 안위하시나이다. (시편 23:4)

Have I not commanded you? Be strong and courageous. Do not be terrified; do not be discouraged, for the LORD your God will be with you wherever you go (Joshua 1:9)

내가 네게 명령한 것이 아니냐 강하고 담대하라 두려워하지 말며 놀라지 말라 네가 어디로 가든지 네 하나님 여호와가 너와 함께 하느니라 하시니라. (여호수아 1:9)

When you pass through the waters, I will be with you; and when you pass through the rivers, they will not sweep over you. When you walk through the fire, you will not be burned; the flames will not set you ablaze. (Isaiah 43:2)

네가 물 가운데로 지날 때에 내가 함께 할 것이라 강을 건널 때에 물이 너를 침몰하지 못할 것이며 네가 불 가운데로 지날 때에 타지도 아니할 것이요 불꽃이 너를 사르지도 못하리니. (이사야 43:2)

(Genesis 6:9) **account** 계산, 계정, 계좌, 계보, 설명하다, 원인이 되다
/ the Great Account 최후의 심판
(Deuteronomy 31:8) **forsake**(= give up, abandon) 버리다, 포기하다
(Psalm 23:4) **comfort** 위로, 위문, 위안, 편안함, 위로(위문)하다
(Isaiah 43:2) **sweep** (빗자루 등으로) 쓸다, 휩쓸다 / **ablaze** 화염에 싸여서, 타오르는

영어성경 말씀을 한글로 해석해 보기

앞서 배운 성경말씀을 소리 내어 읽어보고 해석해 보세요!!

When Enoch had lived 65 years, he became the father of Methuselah. And after he became the father of Methuselah, Enoch walked with God 300 years and had other sons and daughters. (Genesis 5:21~22)

This is the account of Noah. Noah was a righteous man, blameless among the people of his time, and he walked with God. (Genesis 6:9)

The LORD himself goes before you and will be with you; he will never leave you nor forsake you. Do not be afraid; do not be discouraged. (Deuteronomy 31:8)

Even though I walk through the valley of the shadow of death, I will fear no evil, for you are with me; your rod and your staff, they comfort me. (Psalm 23:4)

Have I not commanded you? Be strong and courageous. Do not be terrified; do not be discouraged, for the LORD your God will be with you wherever you go (Joshua 1:9)

When you pass through the waters, I will be with you; and when you pass through the rivers, they will not sweep over you. When you walk through the fire, you will not be burned; the flames will not set you ablaze. (Isaiah 43:2)

Puzzle 10

👫👫 'YOU WILL NEVER WALK ALONE' 에서 배웠던 단어들로 퍼즐을 완성해 봅시다!

가로열쇠
- ③ 산
- ⑥ 계곡
- ⑦ 눈물, 울음, 잡아 뜯다
- ⑨ 믿음, 신앙
- ⑫ 놀라움, 놀라운 것, 경이로움
  - ▶ seven _____s 세계 7대 불가사의
- ⑭ 혼자, 홀로
  - ▶ Better be _____ than in bad company
- ⑮ 사막
- ⑯ 햇살, 햇빛
- ⑰ 웃음
- ⑱ (공간 또는 시간상 떨어져 있는) 거리

세로열쇠
- ❶ 수고, 노력, 노동, 근로
- ❷ 인생, 삶, 생명
- ❸ 실수, 잘못
- ❹ 좁은길 < road
- ❺ 넓은길 > path
- ❽ 건너서, 가로질러
- ❿ 아픔, 수고 ▶ No _____s no gains.
- ⓫ 마주치다, 얼굴
- ⓭ (하늘에서 내리는) 비
- ⓯ 깊이, 형용사는 deep
- ⓰ 가파른, 경사진 ▶ mountain so _____
- ⓳ 차가운 ↔ hot

정답은 책의 뒤편에서 확인하세요

MEMO

You raise me up

When I am down and, oh my soul, so weary
When troubles come and my heart burdened be
Then I am still and wait here in the silence
Until you come and sit awhile with me

(refrain) You raise me up so I can stand on mountains
You raise me up to walk on stormy seas
I am strong when I am on your shoulders
You raise me up to more than I can be

There is no life - no life without it's hunger
Each restless heart beats so imperfectly
But when you come I am filled with wonder
Sometimes, I think I glimpse eternity

------- refrain ×2 -------

You raise me up to more than I can be

◇ QR코드를 스캔하여 유튜브로 들어보세요!!
◇ 유튜브(www.youtube.com) 검색창에 아래와 같이 입력하고 돋보기를
클릭해도 됩니다.

You raise me up secret garden

🎙 노래 알아보기

지치고 힘들 때 하나님께서 나에게 오셔서 나를 일으켜 주신다는 이 노래는 유명한 소설가이자 CCM 작곡가인 브랜든 그래험(Brendon Graham, 1945~)이 작사를 하였고, 그룹 시크릿 가든(Secret Garden)의 멤버이자 음악박사인 롤프 뢰블란(Rolf Lovland, 1955~)이 북아일랜드의 전통 민요인 런던데리 에어(Londonderry Air)를 바탕으로 작곡하였으며, 2001년 발표된 시크릿가든의 4집 앨범인 'Once in a Red Moon'에 최초로 수록된 곡입니다.

이 노래는 이후 조시 그로번(Josh Groban), 웨스트 라이프(West Life), 외판원에서 노래경연 대회를 통해 단숨에 유명인사가 된 폴 포츠(Paul Potts), 셀틱 우먼(Celtic Women), 셀라(Shelah), 귀여운 소녀가수인 코니 텔봇(Conie Telbot) 등 유명한 여러 가수 또는 그룹들이 리메이크(re-make)하여 불렀습니다.

의기소침해 있는 아이를(우리를) 아빠가(하나님이) 안아주고 무등을 태워주는 모습이 상상되는 노래입니다.

🎵 노래 배우기

When I am down and, oh my soul, so weary

when ~ 할 때
down 기분이 침울한, 아래로 ↔ **up** 기분이 좋아진, 위로
oh (감탄사) 오, 아, 저런
soul 영혼 ↔ **body** 육체
▶ 속담 Brevity is the soul of wit 간결함은 재치의 영혼
weary (몹시)지친, 피곤한 ▶ weary of ~ ~에 싫증 난 ▶ dog-weary 아주 지친

When troubles come and my heart burdened be

trouble 문제, 곤란, 병
come 오다 (come-came-come)
heart 마음, 심장
burden 짐, 짐을 진 ▶ my heart burdened be = my heart is burdened 내 마음에 짐이 지워져 있다

Then I am still and wait here in the silence

then 그러면, 그다음에, 그때
still 움직이지 않는, 조용한(quiet), 잠잠한, 계속해서, 아직도
▶ 속담 Still waters runs deep 잠잠한 물이 깊이 흐른다(익은 벼일수록 고개 숙인다, 사려 깊은 사람은 말이 적다, Empty vessels make the most sound)

▶ **stilly** 고요히, 잠잠히
wait 기다리다 ▶ wait a minute(second) 잠시 기다려
here 여기 ↔ **there** 저기
silence 고요, 침묵 ▶ **silent** 고요한, 말이 없는 ▶ holy night silent night 거룩한 밤 고요한 밤

Until you come and sit awhile with me

until (~할 때)까지
sit 앉다 (sit-sat-sat) ▶ **seat** 앉히다 (seat-seated-seated)
awhile 잠시, 잠깐 ▶ **for awhile** 잠시 동안
with ~ 과 같이(함께), ~을 가지고 ▶ **with me** 나와 함께(같이)
　　▶ **with spoon** 스푼을 가지고 ▶ **with grateful heart** 감사하는 마음으로

(refrain) You raise me up so I can stand on mountains

refrain 후렴
raise (위로)들어올리다, (수준을)높이다, (작물을)기르다
~ so (that) I can - : ~ 해서 내가 - 가능하도록 하다
stand 서다 ▶ stand up 서 있다 ▶ stand by 대기하다
mountain 산 > hill 언덕(작은 산)
mountains 산맥, 산들 ▶ The Rocky Mountains 록키 산맥

You raise me up to walk on stormy seas

walk 걷다 < run 뛰다
stormy sea 폭풍치는 바다 ▶ storm 폭풍

I am strong when I am on your shoulders

strong 힘센 ▶ strength 힘
shoulder 어깨 ▶ head and shoulders knees and toes knees toes 머리 어깨 무릎 발 무릎 발

You raise me up to more than I can be

more than ~ ~보다
I can be 내가 가능한 상태

There is no life - no life without it's hunger;

life 삶, 생활, 생명 ↔ death 사망, 죽음
without 없이 ↔ with 가지고

▶ 속담 There is no smoke without fire 불없이 연기 없다(아니땐 굴뚝에 연기나랴)
hunger 배고픔, (~에 대한)갈망 ▶ hungry 배고픈, 굶주리는

Each restless heart beats so imperfectly;

restless 쉼(휴식) 없는 ▶ rest 쉼(휴식)
▶ restless wanderer 쉼 없는 유랑자
▶ less 는 명사 뒤에 붙어서 ~ 이 없는 이라고 해석 됩니다 (pain ↔ painless)
beat 고동(치다), 때리다 , 박자 ▶ heart beat 심장 박동
imperfectly 불완전하게 ↔ perfectly 완전하게
▶ im 은 명사나 부사등 앞에 붙어서 반대의 의미를 나타냅니다 (possible ↔ impossible)
▶ 속담 Practice makes perfect 연습하면 완벽해진다

But when you come I am filled with wonder,

fill 채우다 ▶ be filled with ~ ~으로 채워지다
wonder 놀라움, 놀라운 것 ▶ seven wonders 세계 7대 불가사의

Sometimes, I think I glimpse eternity

sometimes 어떤 때는
think 생각하다 ▶ thought(=thinking) 생각
glimpse 언뜻 보다, 잠깐보다 ▶ catch(have, get) a glimpse of ~ ~을 어렴풋이 알다
eternity 영원, 오랜 시간 ▶ eternal 영원한 ▶ eternal life 영생

refrain

You raise me up to more than I can be

노래 배우기(REmind)

아래와 같이 앞서 배웠던 단어나 문구의 뜻을 말해보고 각자 문장을 만들어 보세요!!

When I am down and, oh my soul, so weary

when *~ 할 때*
down *기분이 침울한, 아래로* ↔ **up** *기분이 좋아진, 위로*
oh *감탄사 오, 아*

soul 영혼 ↔ **body** 육체
▶ 속담 Brevity is the soul of wit *간결함은 재치의 영혼*
weary *지친, 피곤한* ▶ weary of ~ *~에 싫증 난* ▶ dog-weary *아주 지친*

When troubles come and my heart burdened be

trouble
come   (come-   -come)
heart
burden

Then I am still and wait here in the silence

then
still   ▶ **stilly**
▶ 속담 Still water runs
wait   ▶ wait a minute(second)
here   ↔ there
silence   ▶ silent   ▶ holy night silent night

Until you come and sit awhile with me

until
sit   (sit-sat-sat) ▶ seat   (seat-seated-seated)
awhile   ▶ for awhile
with me   ▶ with spoon   ▶ with grateful heart

(refrain) You raise me up so I can stand on mountains

refrain

raise
~ so (that) I can -
stand   ▶ stand up   ▶ stand by
mountain   > hill
mountains   ▶ The Rocky Mountains __

You raise me up to walk on stormy seas

walk   < run
stormy sea   ▶ storm

I am strong when I am on your shoulders

strong ▶ strength
shoulder
▶ head and shoulders knees and toes knees toes

You raise me up to more than I can be

more than ~
I can be

There is no life - no life without it's hunger;

life ↔ death
without ↔ with
There is no smoke without
hunger ▶ hungry

Each restless heart beats so imperfectly;

restless ▶ rest ▶ restless wanderer
pain ↔ painless
beat ▶ heart beat
imperfectly ↔ perfectly
▶ **impossible** ↔ possible
▶ 속담 Practice makes perfect

But when you come I am filled with wonder,

fill ▶ be filled with ~
wonder ▶ seven wonders

Sometimes, I think I glimpse eternity

sometimes
think ▶ thought(=thinking)
glimpse ▶ catch(have, get) a glimpse of ~
eternity ▶ eternal ▶ eternal life

refrain
You raise me up to more than I can be

When I am down and, oh my soul, so weary

내가 침울하고, 오 나의 영혼이 매우 지쳐 있을 때

When troubles come and my heart burdened be

문제들이 다가오고, 나의 마음에 짐이 지워진 듯할 때

Then I am still and wait here in the silence

그러면 나는 가만히 여기 침묵 속에 기다립니다

Until you come and sit awhile with me

당신(하나님)이 (나에게) 와서 내 옆에 잠시 앉아계실 때까지

(refrain)

(후렴)

You raise me up so I can stand on mountains

당신은 내가 산맥 위에 서 있을 수 있도록 나를 올려 주십니다

You raise me up to walk on stormy seas

당신은 내가 폭풍 치는 바다들 위를 걸을 수 있도록 나를 높여주십니다

I am strong when I am on your shoulders

나는 당신의 어깨위에 있을 때 강합니다

You raise me up to more than I can be

당신은 내가 가능한 상태 보다 나를 높여 주십니다

There is no life - no life without it's hunger;

갈급함(배고픔)이 없는 삶은 없습니다

Each restless heart beats so imperfectly;

각자의 쉼없는 심장은 그렇게도 불완전하게 고동치고 있습니다

But when you come I am filled with wonder,

그러나 당신이 (나에게) 오면 나는 놀라움으로 채워지게 됩니다

Sometimes, I think I glimpse eternity,

어떤 때는 나는 영원을 어렴풋이 본다는 생각을 합니다

refrain × 2

후렴 × 2

You raise me up to more than I can be

당신은 내가 가능한 상태 보다 나를 높여 주십니다

* 상기 번역은 영어공부를 위한 해석(직역)이며 공인된 한글 번역곡(가사)은 아님을 알려드립니다

번역해보기

When I am down and, oh my soul, so weary

내가 침울하고, 오 나의 영혼이 매우 지쳐 있을 때

When troubles come and my heart burdened be

Then I am still and wait here in the silence

Until you come and sit awhile with me

(refrain)

You raise me up so I can stand on mountains

You raise me up to walk on stormy seas

I am strong when I am on your shoulders

You raise me up to more than I can be

There is no life - no life without it's hunger;

갈급함(배고픔)이 없는 삶은 없습니다

Each restless heart beats so imperfectly;

But when you come I am filled with wonder,

Sometimes, I think I glimpse eternity,

refrain × 2

You raise me up to more than I can be

✝ 노래와 관련된 성경 말씀

앞서 배운 영어찬양과 관련된 성경말씀을 알아봅시다!!

"This is the will of Him who sent Me, that of all that He has given Me I lose nothing, but raise it up on the last day. For my Father's will is that everyone who looks to the Son and believes in him shall have eternal life, and I will raise them up at the last day.
(John 6:39~40)

나를 보내신 이의 뜻은 내게 주신 자 중에 내가 하나도 잃어버리지 아니하고 마지막 날에 다시 살리는 이것이니라. 내 아버지의 뜻은 아들을 보고 믿는 자마다 영생을 얻는 이것이니 마지막 날에 내가 이를 다시 살리리라 하시니라. (요한복음 6:39~40)

No one can come to Me unless the Father who sent Me draws him; and I will raise him up on the last day. (John 6:44)

나를 보내신 아버지께서 이끌지 아니하시면 아무도 내게 올 수 없으니 오는 그를 내가 마지막 날에 다시 살리리라. (요한복음 6:44)

Come to me, all you who are weary and burdened, and I will give you rest.
(Matthew 11:28)

수고하고 무거운 짐 진 자들아 다 내게로 오라 내가 너희를 쉬게 하리라. (마태복음 11:28)

Even though I walk through the valley of the shadow of death, I will fear no evil, for you are with me; your rod and your staff, they comfort me. (Psalm 23:4)

내가 사망의 음침한 골짜기로 다닐지라도 해를 두려워하지 않을것은 주께서 나와 함께 하심이라 주의 지팡이와 막대기가 나를 안위하시나이다. (시편 23:4)

Here I am! I stand at the door and knock. If anyone hears my voice and opens the door, I will come in and eat with him, and he with me.
To him who overcomes, I will give the right to sit with me on my throne, just as I overcame and sat down with my Father on his throne. (Revelation 3:20)

볼지어다 내가 문 밖에 서서 두드리노니 누구든지 내 음성을 듣고 문을 열면 내가 그에게로 들어가 그와 더불어 먹고 그는 나와 더불어 먹으리라 이기는 그에게는 내가 내 보좌에 함께 앉게 하여 주기를 내가 이기고 아버지 보좌에 함께 앉은 것과 같이 하리라 (요한계시록 3:20)

🔊 영어성경 말씀을 한글로 해석해 보기

앞서 배운 성경말씀을 소리 내어 읽어보고 해석해 보세요!!

"This is the will of Him who sent Me, that of all that He has given Me I lose nothing, but raise it up on the last day. For my Father's will is that everyone who looks to the Son and believes in him shall have eternal life, and I will raise them up at the last day.
(John 6:39~40)

No one can come to Me unless the Father who sent Me draws him; and I will raise him up on the last day. (John 6:44)

Come to me, all you who are weary and burdened, and I will give you rest. (Matthew 11:28)

Even though I walk through the valley of the shadow of death, I will fear no evil, for you are with me; your rod and your staff, they comfort me. (Psalm 23:4)

Here I am! I stand at the door and knock. If anyone hears my voice and opens the door, I will come in and eat with him, and he with me.
To him who overcomes, I will give the right to sit with me on my throne, just as I overcame and sat down with my Father on his throne. (Revelation 3:20)

Puzzle 11

'YOU RAISE ME UP' 에서 배웠던 단어들로 퍼즐을 완성해 봅시다!

Across_가로

5 고요, 침묵
7 폭풍, 폭풍우
8 완전한, 완벽한
9 기다리다
  ▶ _____ a minute 잠시 기다려줘
11 걷다 < run
13 어깨
14 짐, 짐을 진
15 쉼(휴식) 없는

Down_세로

1 (위로)들어올리다, (작물을)기르다
2 여기 ↔ there
3 배고픔, (~에 대한)갈망
4 언뜻 보다, 잠깐 보다
6 영혼 ↔ body
7 움직이지 않는, 조용한, 계속해서, 아직도
  ▶ _____ waters runs deep 잠잠한 물이 깊이 흐른다
10 문제, 곤란, 병
11 없이 ↔ with
  ▶ There is no smoke _____ fire
12 (몹시)지친, 피곤한

정답은 책의 뒤편에서 확인하세요

Joy to the world the Lord has come

Joy to the world! The Lord has come
Let earth receive her King!
Let every heart prepare Him room

And heaven and nature sing ×2
And heaven, and heaven and nature sing

Joy to the world! the Savior reigns
Let men their songs employ
While fields and floods; Rocks, hills and plains

Repeat the sounding joy ×2
Repeat, repeat the sounding joy

No more let sin and sorrow grow
Nor thorns infest the ground
He comes to make; His blessings flow

Far as the curse is found ×2
Far as, far as the curse is found

He rules the world with truth and grace
And makes the nations prove
The glories of His righteousness

And wonders of His love ×2
And wonders and wonders of His love

◇ QR코드를 스캔하여 유튜브로 들어보세요!!
◇ 유튜브(www.youtube.com) 검색창에 아래와 같이 입력하고 돋보기를 클릭해도 됩니다.

Joy to the world the Lord has come 🔍

🎙 노래 알아보기

우리가 잘 알고 있는 크리스마스 캐럴(Christmas carol)이며 찬송가 115장인 이곡은 아이작 왓츠 (Isaac Watts, 1674~1748)의 찬송시에 로웰 메이슨(Lowell Mason, 1792~1872)이 곡을 붙여 만들었습니다. 이곡의 작사자인 아이작 왓츠(Isaac Watts) 목사님은 성경의 시편 98장을 기반으로 이 곡을 썼다고 합니다. 왓츠는 영국에서 태어났고 에딘버러(Edinburgh) 대학에서 신학박사 학위를 받았으며, 교육자, 목회자이며 찬송시 작사자로 유명합니다. 당시 성경 시편을 변형하지 않고 그대로 찬송으로 부르던 시대에 700여 편의 은혜롭고 아름다운 음율의 찬송시를 작곡하여 전파함으로써 와츠는 영국 찬송가의 아버지라고도 불리고 있습니다.

이 곡의 작곡가 로웰 메이슨(Lowell Mason, 1792~1872)은 1836년 이곡을 작곡했습니다. 메이슨은 처음에는 양복점에서 일하다가 은행가가 되었지만, 음악에 소질이 있어서 교회에서 성가대 지휘자와 오르간반주자로 활동하면서 여러 교회음악을 작곡하였습니다. 메이슨은 처음에는 이름을 숨기고 작곡했지만, 점점 많은 교회의 음악감독을 맡게 되었습니다. 우리가 잘 알고 있는 찬송가 338장 '내주를 가까이 하게 함은(Nearer My God to Thee)'도 메이슨이 작곡한 곡입니다.

메이슨은 'Joy to the World'의 음률을 헨델(George Frederick Handel, 1685~1759)의 유명한 클래식 음악인 메시아(Messia)에서 리듬을 빌려와 작곡하였다 합니다.

우리에게 친숙한 바로크시대 음악가인 헨델은 50대 중반에 자신이 운영하던 극장의 파산과 질병으로 크게 고통 받고 있던 중 비참하고 낙담한 상태에서 굳은 결의로 기도를 시작했으며 기도 중 받은 영감으로 24일이라는 짧은 기간 동안 기적적으로 260페이지에 달하는 3부작 '메시아'를 완성하였고, 완성된 악보(manuscript)의 가장 마지막에는 하나님 홀로 영광 받으소서(SDG, Soli Deo Gloria, To God alone the glory) 라고 적었다 합니다. 이곡과 함께 헨델의 메시아도 같이 들어보길 바랍니다.

🎵 노래 배우기

Joy to the World, the Lord has come

joy 기쁨 ▶ joyful 기쁜, 아주 기뻐하는 ▶ Joy to ~ ~에 기쁨을(기쁨이 있을 지어다)
world 세상, 세계
Lord (대문자로 써서)하나님, 군주, 영주
come 오다(come-came-come)

Let earth receive her King;

let ~ ~을 하게 하다, 시키다 ▶ let me introduce myself 제 소개를 하겠습니다

earth 땅, 지구 ↔ heaven 하늘, 천국
receive 환영하다, 받다, 받아들이다 ↔ serve 주다, 제공하다, 이바지하다
her 그녀의, 여기서는 땅을 여성으로 표현하여
king 왕 ▶ queen 왕비

Let every heart prepare Him room,

every 모든 ▶ every word 모든 말 ▶ every part 모든 부분
heart 마음, 심장 ▶ heart beat 심장 박동
prepare 준비하다, 대비하다 ▶ preparation 준비, 대비
Him 그의
room 방 ▶ family room(= living room) 거실

And Heaven and nature sing,

heaven 천국, 하늘 ↔ earth 지구, 땅
nature 자연, 천성, 본성 ▶ divine nature 신성한 성품 ▶ natural 자연스러운, 타고난
sing 노래하다(=sing-sang-sung) ▶ singer 가수

And Heaven and nature sing,
And Heaven, and Heaven, and nature sing.
Joy to the World, the Savior reigns!

savior 구세주, 구원자
reign 다스리다, 다스리는 기간, 통치 (=rule)

Let men their songs employ

their 그들의 ▶ they 그들
song 노래 ▶ sing 노래하다
employ 이용하다(use), 고용하다

While fields and floods; Rocks, hills and plains

while ~까지, ~하는 동안
field 들판, 경기장, 분야 ▶ green field 푸른 들판 ▶ golf field 골프 경기장
flood 밀물, 홍수, 큰(강)물 ▶ Noah's Ark and the great Flood 노아의 방주와 대홍수
rock 바위 ▶ rocky 바위가 많은, 바위의
hill 동산(낮은 산) < mountain 산(높은 산)

plains 평야, 평원, 평지 ▶ plain 분명한, 솔직한, 평범한
▶ plain yoghurt (과일, 설탕 등) 다른 것을 넣지 않은 요구르트

Repeat the sounding joy

repeat 반복하다, 되풀이하다, 따라하다 ▶ listen and repeat 듣고 따라하세요
▶ repeat a refrain ▶ 후렴구를 반복하세요
sounding 소리나는, 울려퍼지는, (의견)조사 ▶ sounding bell 울려퍼지는 종 ▶
▶ resounding (길게) 울려퍼지는 ▶ resounding gong 길게 울려퍼지는 징

Repeat the sounding joy
Repeat, repeat the sounding joy
No more let sin and sorrow grow

let 허락하다 ▶ let me introduce myself 나를 소개하도록 허락해 주세요
sin 죄, 죄악, 잘못 ▶ sinful 죄가 되는, 나쁜
sorrow (매우 큰) 슬픔, (매우) 슬픈 일, 슬퍼하다,

Nor thorns infest the ground

nor ~도(또한) 아니다
thorn 식물의 가시, 가시나무
infest (곤충, 쥐, 병 등 안 좋은 것이) 들끓다, 우글거리다
ground 땅, 토양, 지면, 근거
ground infested with thorn 가시나무로 뒤덮여 있는 땅

He comes to make His blessings flow

come to make ~ ~ 을 만들기 위하여 오다
blessing 축복, 허락 ▶ bless 축복하다
▶ God bless you! 그대에게 하나님의 축복이 있기를!
flow (물 등의)흐름, 흐르다, 몰입

Far as the curse is found

far 먼, 멀리 ▶ far from~ ~로부터 먼
far as ~ ~ 까지 ▶ as far as ~ 하는 한
curse 저주, 골칫거리, 악담
found 찾았다(find-found-found)

Far as the curse is found
Far as, far as the curse is found
He rules the world with truth and grace

rule 통치하다(=reign), 다스리다, 규칙, 원칙 ▶ ruler (길이를 재는 경우 사용하는) 자
truth 진실, 진리 ↔ falsehood 거짓, 가짜
▶ true 진짜인, 사실인, 맞는 ↔ false 가짜인, 가짜의, 거짓의
▶ 속담 The truth will come out 진실은 드러나게 마련이다
grace 은혜, 은총, 우아함, 품위, 예의, 식사전 기도 ▶ grace of God 신의 은혜(은총)

And makes the nations prove

nation 나라, 국가, 민족
prove 입증하다, 증명하다, 드러나다 ▶ It will prove true 그것은 사실임이 드러날 것 이다

The glories of His righteousness

glory 영광, 영애, 찬양
▶ Glory to God in the highest 지극히 높은곳에 계신 하느님께 영광
righteousness 의로움, 정의, 정도, 공의 ▶ righteous 의로운, 옳은, 정의로운, 당연한
▶ path of righteousness 의(義)의 길
▶ What if there are five righteous people in the city? 그 도시에 다섯 명의 의인이 있다면 어떻게 하시겠습니까?

And wonders of His love

wonder 놀라움, 경이로운(것), 궁금해하다
▶ the wonders of modern technology 현대 과학기술의 경이
love 사랑, 애정, 사랑하다
He makes the nations prove the glories of His righteousness and wonders of His love
그는 나라들이 그의 의의 영광과 그의 사랑의 놀라움을 드러내도록 만드신다

And wonders of His love
And wonders and wonders of His love

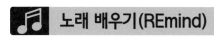 **노래 배우기(REmind)**

아래와 같이 앞서 배웠던 단어나 문구의 뜻을 말해보고 각자 문장을 만들어 보세요!!

Joy to the World, the Lord has come

joy *기쁨* ▶ **joyful** *기쁜* ▶ **Joy to** ~ *~에 기쁨을*
world *세상, 세계*
Lord *(대문자로 써서)하나님, 군주, 영주*
come *오다* (come-came-come)

Let earth receive her King;

let	▶ let me introduce myself	
earth	↔ heaven	
receive	↔ serve	
her		
king	▶ queen	

Let every heart prepare Him room,

every	▶ every word	▶ every part
heart	▶ heart beat	
prepare	▶ preparation	
Him		
room	▶ family room (= _____)	

And Heaven and nature sing,

heaven	↔	
nature	▶ divine nature	▶ natural
sing	(= sing - _____ - sung)	▶ singer

And Heaven and nature sing,
And Heaven, and Heaven, and nature sing.
Joy to the World, the Savior reigns!

savior
reign ▶ rule

Let men their songs employ

their ▶ they

song ▶ sing

employ

While fields and floods; Rocks, hills and plains

while

field ▶ green field ▶ golf field

flood ▶ Noah's Ark and the Great Flood

rock ▶ rocky

hill < mountain

plains ▶ plain ▶ plain yoghurt

Repeat the sounding joy

repeat ▶ listen and repeat ▶ repeat a refrain

sounding ▶ sounding bell

▶ **resounding** ▶ resounding gong

Repeat the sounding joy
Repeat, repeat the sounding joy
No more let sin and sorrow grow

let ▶ let me introduce my self

sin ▶ sinful

sorrow

Nor thorns infest the ground

nor

thorn

infest

ground ▶ ground infested with thorn

He comes to make His blessings flow

come to make

blessing ▶ bless

▶ God bless you!

flow

Far as the curse is found

far _____ ▶ far from~ _____
far as _____ ▶ as far as _____
curse _____
found _____ (find - _____ - _____)

Far as the curse is found
Far as, far as the curse is found
He rules the world with truth and grace

rule _____ ▶ ruler _____
truth _____ ↔ _____
▶ **true** _____ ↔ _____
▶ 속담 The truth will come out
grace _____ ▶ grace of God _____

And makes the nations prove

nation _____
prove _____ ▶ It will prove true _____

The glories of His righteousness

glory _____
▶ Glory to God in the highest _____
righteousness _____ ▶ righteous _____
▶ path of righteousness _____
▶ What if there are five _____ people in the city?

And wonders of His love

wonder _____
▶ the wonders of modern technology _____

And wonders of His love
And wonders and wonders of His love

Joy to the world! The Lord has come	세상에 기쁨 있으라 주님이 오셨다
Let earth receive her King!	땅이여 그녀의 왕을 환영할 준비를 하라
Let every heart prepare Him room	모든 마음은 그를 위한 방을 마련하라
And heaven and nature sing	그리고 하늘과 자연은 노래하라
And heaven and nature sing	그리고 하늘과 자연은 노래하라
And heaven, and heaven and nature sing	그리고 하늘과 자연은 노래하라
Joy to the world! the Savior reigns	세상에 기쁨 있으라 구세주가 다스리신다
Let men their songs employ	모든 사람들은 노래할 지어다
While fields and floods; Rocks, hills and plains	들과 강까지; 바위, 언덕, 그리고 평야(까지)
Repeat the sounding joy	반복하라 울려 퍼지는 기쁨을
Repeat the sounding joy	반복하라 울려 퍼지는 기쁨을
Repeat, repeat the sounding joy	반복하라 반복하라 울려 퍼지는 기쁨을
No more let sin and sorrow grow	더 이상 죄와 슬픔이 자라지 못하도록 하라
Nor thorns infest the ground	또한 가시나무가 땅을 뒤덮지 못하도록 하라
He comes to make; His blessings flow	그는 그의 축복이 넘쳐흐르게 하려고 오신다
Far as the curse is found	멀리까지라도 문제가 발견되는
Far as the curse is found	멀리까지라도 문제가 발견되는
Far as, far as the curse is found	멀리까지라도 멀리까지라도 문제가 발견되는
He rules the world with truth and grace	그는 진실과 은혜로 세상을 다스리신다
And makes the nations prove	그리고 나라들이 드러내도록 만드신다
The glories of His righteousness	그의 의로움의 영광을
And wonders of His love	그리고 그의 사랑의 놀라움을
And wonders of His love	그리고 그의 사랑의 놀라움을
And wonders and wonders of His love	그리고 그의 사랑의 놀라움을 놀라움을

＊ 상기 번역은 영어공부를 위한 해석(직역)이며 공인된 한글 번역곡(가사)은 아님을 알려드립니다

번역해보기

Joy to the world! The Lord has come

세상에 기쁨 있으라 주님이 오셨다

Let earth receive her King!

Let every heart prepare Him room

And heaven and nature sing

And heaven and nature sing

And heaven, and heaven and nature sing

Joy to the world! the Savior reigns

Let men their songs employ

While fields and floods; Rocks, hills and plains

Repeat the sounding joy

Repeat the sounding joy

Repeat, repeat the sounding joy

No more let sin and sorrow grow

더 이상 죄와 슬픔이 자라지 못하도록 하라

Nor thorns infest the ground

He comes to make; His blessings flow

Far as the curse is found

Far as the curse is found

Far as, far as the curse is found

He rules the world with truth and grace

And makes the nations prove

The glories of His righteousness

And wonders of His love

And wonders of His love

And wonders and wonders of His love

✚ 노래와 관련된 성경 말씀

앞서 배운 영어찬양과 관련된 성경말씀을 알아봅시다!!

But the angel said to them, "Do not be afraid. I bring you good news of great joy that will be for all the people. (Luke 2:10)

천사가 이르되 무서워하지 말라 보라 내가 온 백성에게 미칠 큰 기쁨의 좋은 소식을 너희에게 전하노라.
(누가복음 2:10)

He came to that which was his own, but his own did not receive him.
Yet to all who received him, to those who believed in his name, he gave the right to become children of God - children born not of natural descent, nor of human decision or a husband's will, but born of God.
The Word became flesh and made his dwelling among us. We have seen his glory, the glory of the One and Only, who came from the Father, full of grace and truth. (John 1:11~14)

자기 땅에 오매 자기 백성이 영접하지 아니하였으나
영접하는 자 곧 그 이름을 믿는 자들에게는 하나님의 자녀가 되는 권세를 주셨으니 이는 혈통으로나 육정으로나 사람의 뜻으로 나지 아니하고 오직 하나님께로부터 난 자들이니라
말씀이 육신이 되어 우리 가운데 거하시매 우리가 그의 영광을 보니 아버지의 독생자의 영광이요 은혜와 진리가 충만하더라. (요한복음 1:11~14)

"For God so loved the world that he gave his one and only Son, that whoever believes in him shall not perish but have eternal life. (John 3:16)

"For God so loved the world that he gave his one and only Son, that whoever believes in him shall not perish but have eternal life. (John 3:16)
하나님이 세상을 이처럼 사랑하사 독생자를 주셨으니 이는 그를 믿는 자마다 멸망하지 않고 영생을 얻게 하려 하심이라. (요한복음 3:16)

But the fruit of the Spirit is love, joy, peace, patience, kindness, goodness, faithfulness, gentleness and self-control. Against such things there is no law. (Galatians 5:22~23)

오직 성령의 열매는 사랑과 희락과 화평과 오래 참음과 자비와 양선과 충성과 온유와 절제니 이같은 것을 금지할 법이 없느니라. (갈라디아서 5:22~23)

(John 1:13) **descent** 하강, 급습, 내리막, 혈통, 상속
(John 1:14) **flesh** 살(뼈나 가죽과 대비하여), 육체, 육욕, 정욕
        dwelling 집, 거주지, 주소
(John 3:16) **perish** 멸망하다, 전사하다 /
        He who lives by the sword will perish by the sword 칼로 흥한 자는 칼로 망한다.

🗣️)) 영어성경 말씀을 한글로 해석해 보기

앞서 배운 성경말씀을 소리 내어 읽어보고 해석해 보세요!!

But the angel said to them, "Do not be afraid. I bring you good news of great joy that will be for all the people. (Luke 2:10)

He came to that which was his own, but his own did not receive him.
Yet to all who received him, to those who believed in his name, he gave the right to become children of God - children born not of natural descent, nor of human decision or a husband's will, but born of God.
The Word became flesh and made his dwelling among us. We have seen his glory, the glory of the One and Only, who came from the Father, full of grace and truth. (John 1:11~14)

"For God so loved the world that he gave his one and only Son, that whoever believes in him shall not perish but have eternal life. (John 3:16)

But the fruit of the Spirit is love, joy, peace, patience, kindness, goodness, faithfulness, gentleness and self-control. Against such things there is no law. (Galatians 5:22~23)

Puzzle 12

♫ 'JOY TO THE WORLD, THE LORD HAS COME' 에서 배웠던 단어들로 퍼즐을 완성해 봅시다!

Across_가로	Down_세로
② 축복하다 ▶ God _____ you! 당신에게 하나님의 축복이 있기를!	① 환영하다, 받다, 받아들이다 ↔ serve 주다, 제공하다
⑥ 방 ▶ family _____ 거실	③ 동산(낮은 산) < mountain 산(높은 산)
⑧ 영광, 영애, 찬양	④ (매우 큰) 슬픔, (매우) 슬픈 일, 슬퍼하다,
⑨ 준비하다, 대비하다	⑤ 기쁨
⑩ 세상, 세계	⑦ 자연, 천성, 본성
⑫ 다스리다, 다스리는 기간, 통치 (=rule)	⑧ 땅, 토양, 지면, 근거
⑬ 입증하다, 증명하다, 드러나다	⑪ 안으로 ↔ OUT 밖으로
	⑭ 바위 ▶ _____ - scissor - paper

MEMO

APPENDIX

A friend in need is a friend indeed	필요할 때 친구가 진정한 친구
All that's fair must fade	아름다운 것은 모두 반드시 시들기 마련이다
A sound mind in a sound body	건강한 신체에 건전한 정신
A stitch in time saves nine = There is a time for everything	적당한 때 한 땀이 아홉 땀의 수고를 덜어준다
After a storm comes a calm	폭풍우 후에 고요함이 온다(苦盡甘來, 고진감래)
Art is long, life is short	예술은 길고, 인생은 짧다
As long as there's life, there's hope	생명이 있는 한 희망이 있다
Ask, and it shall be given to you	구하라, 그러면 너에게 주어질 것이다
Avarice(Greed) blinds our eyes	탐욕은 우리의 눈을 멀게 한다
Beauty is but(only) skin deep	아름다움은 단지 피부의 두께에 불과하다
= Don't judge a book by its cover	책의 표지로 책을 판단하지 말라
= Never judge someone by their appearance	사람을 그들의 외모로 절대 판단하지 말라
Better be alone than in bad company	나쁜 친구를 사귀는 것보다는 혼자가 낫다
Better late than never	늦는 것이 안 하는 것보다는 낫다
Brevity is the soul of wit	간결함은 재치의 영혼

Don't put new wine into old bottle	새 포도주를 오래된 병에 담지 마라(=새 술은 새 부대에)
He who lives by the sword will perish by the sword	칼에 의해서 사는 자는 칼에 의해서 죽는다 (칼로 흥한 자는 칼로 망한다)
Heaven helps those who help themselves	하늘은 스스로 돕는 자를 돕는다
However humble it may be, there is no place like home	아무리 누추해도 집만 한 곳은 없다
In unity, there is strength	뭉치는 곳에 힘이 있다
It is never too late to learn	배우기에는 절대로 늦지 않다
= It is never too late to mend	고치기에 너무 늦은 때는 절대로 없다
Make hay while the sun shines	해가 비출 때 풀을 말려라 = 기회를 놓치지 말라 = 쇠뿔도 단김에 빼라
Many hands make light work	많은 손이 가벼운 일을 만든다(백지장도 맞들면 낫다)
= Two hands(heads) are better than one	두 개의 손이(머리가) 한 개보다 낫다
Never put off till tomorrow what you can do today	오늘 할 수 있는 것을 내일로 미루지 말라
= Live today as if there's no tomorrow	내일이 없는 것처럼 오늘을 살아라
No pains, no gains	수고 없이 얻는 것이 없다
No rose without a thorn	가시 없는 장미는 없다
= Every rose has its thorn	모든 장미는 그의 가시를 가지고 있다
Practice makes perfect	연습하면 완벽해진다
Praises can make even a whale dance	칭찬은 고래까지도 춤추게 한다
Still waters run deep	잠잠한 물이 깊이 흐른다(=익은 벼일수록 고개 숙인다, 사려 깊은 사람은 말이 적다)

= Empty vessels make the most sound	빈 그릇이 가장 큰 소리를 만든다
The more you learn, the more you earn	더 많이 배울수록 더 많이 번다
The truth will come out	진실은 드러나게(밝혀지게) 마련이다
There is no smoke without fire	불 없이 연기 없다(아니 땐 굴뚝에 연기나랴)
= No smoke, no fire	연기 없이 불 없다
= Where there's no smoke, there's no fire	연기 없는 곳에 불 없다
Time flies like an arrow	세월은 화살과 같이 날아간다(세월은 유수와 같다)
Time and tide wait(s) for no man	세월은 사람을 기다려 주지 않는다
Truth will prevail	진리는 승리한다
Where there is a will, there is a way	뜻이 있는 곳에 길이 있다
While there is life, there is hope	생명이 있는 한 희망이 있다
You get what you pay for	네가 값을 치른 것을 너는 얻는다(=싼 게 비지떡)
= You reap what you sow	네가 심은 것을 너는 거둘 것이다
= As you sow, so shall you reap	심은 대로 너는 거둘 것이다

1ST Draw me close to you

2ND Give Thanks

3RD God will make a way

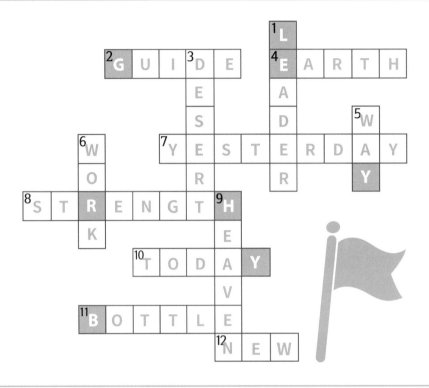

4TH God is the strength of my heart

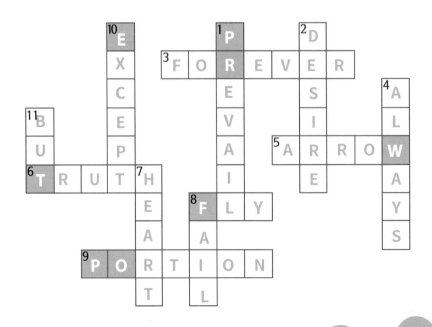

5TH If I come to Jesus

6TH Standing on the Promise

7TH He never sleep

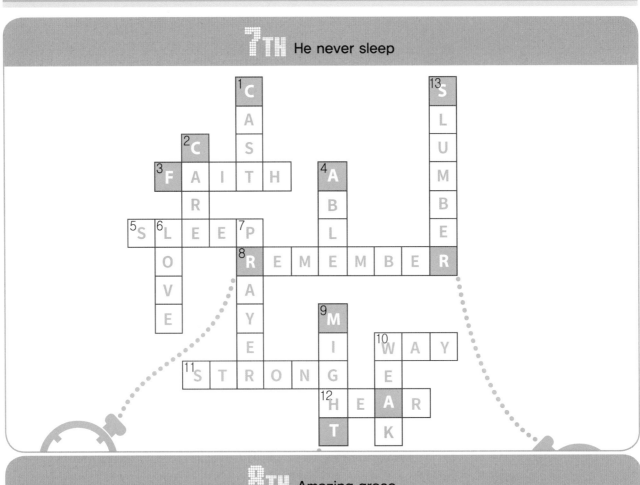

8TH Amazing grace

9TH There is none like You

10TH You will never walk alone

11TH You raise me up

12TH Joy to the world the Lord has come

아름다운 **찬양**으로 배우는 **영어**

글쓴이 • 이철주
도운이 • 이서희, 이건우
감수 • 박은영
발행일 • 2015년 12월 25일
디자인 • 한혜경, 이지연
표지디자인 • 이지연
펴낸이 • 유세연
펴낸곳 • 도서출판 하늘샘
출판등록 • 제367-2015-14호
전화 • 070-7583-2986
e-mail : yusae017@naver.com
http://cafe.naver.com/ccmenglish

© 2015, 이철주
ISBN 979-11-955996-0-8